www.themailboxbooks.com

The Mailbox® Monthly Idea Books— Your Ultimate Monthly Resource!

Your friends at *The Mailbox®* have taken monthly books to a whole new level! We've created a Web site that contains even more classroom resources to complement the hundreds of curriculum-based activities in each book. We've also added skill lines to each idea for a quick curriculum reference at a glance. Plus, every book has a comprehensive index to make planning and selecting activities even easier! All of these terrific features make this series of monthly books one that you can't be without!

Now Internet Interactive!

- For each book, you'll enjoy over **50 pages** of online resources, such as patterns, reproducibles, song cards, and classroom forms!
- You'll find **new** resources for **every** thematic unit in each book!
- Many classroom forms can be **filled out online** and printed. No more handwritten versions!
- Web site content is tailored to you and your **grade level.**
- **All** reproducibles and pattern pages from each monthly book are available online for **easy printing.**
- Access is absolutely **FREE!**

Getting your online extras is as easy as 1, 2, 3!

1. Go to www.themailboxbooks.com and click on "Add a book."
2. Complete the simple registration form.
3. Follow the on-screen instructions to add your book.

Look for the computer icon 🖥 throughout each book to guide you to your FREE online extras.

About This Book

It's hard to believe we could improve on our best-selling series of monthly idea books—but we have! In this edition, you'll find the following exciting new features added to our irreplaceable collection of curriculum-based ideas!

- A Web site containing *even more* classroom resources complements the hundreds of activities provided in each book. (To access this incredible site for free, follow the simple instructions found on page 1.)
- A skill line for each idea provides a curriculum reference at a glance.
- A comprehensive index makes selecting and planning activities a breeze!

We think you'll agree that these new features make this series of monthly books the best ever!

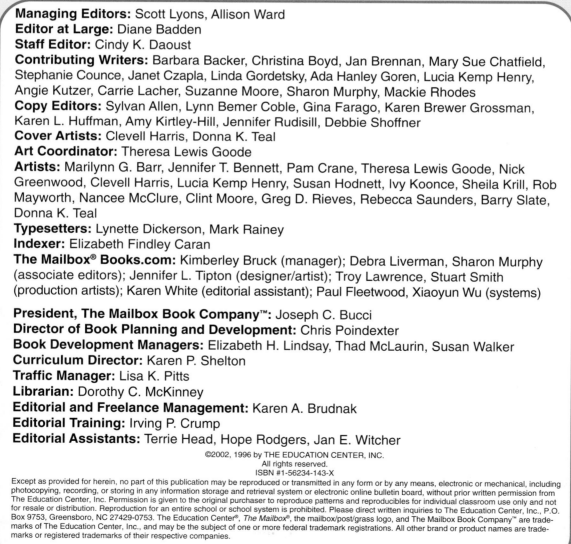

Managing Editors: Scott Lyons, Allison Ward
Editor at Large: Diane Badden
Staff Editor: Cindy K. Daoust
Contributing Writers: Barbara Backer, Christina Boyd, Jan Brennan, Mary Sue Chatfield, Stephanie Counce, Janet Czapla, Linda Gordetsky, Ada Hanley Goren, Lucia Kemp Henry, Angie Kutzer, Carrie Lacher, Suzanne Moore, Sharon Murphy, Mackie Rhodes
Copy Editors: Sylvan Allen, Lynn Bemer Coble, Gina Farago, Karen Brewer Grossman, Karen L. Huffman, Amy Kirtley-Hill, Jennifer Rudisill, Debbie Shoffner
Cover Artists: Clevell Harris, Donna K. Teal
Art Coordinator: Theresa Lewis Goode
Artists: Marilynn G. Barr, Jennifer T. Bennett, Pam Crane, Theresa Lewis Goode, Nick Greenwood, Clevell Harris, Lucia Kemp Henry, Susan Hodnett, Ivy Koonce, Sheila Krill, Rob Mayworth, Nancee McClure, Clint Moore, Greg D. Rieves, Rebecca Saunders, Barry Slate, Donna K. Teal
Typesetters: Lynette Dickerson, Mark Rainey
Indexer: Elizabeth Findley Caran
The Mailbox® Books.com: Kimberley Bruck (manager); Debra Liverman, Sharon Murphy (associate editors); Jennifer L. Tipton (designer/artist); Troy Lawrence, Stuart Smith (production artists); Karen White (editorial assistant); Paul Fleetwood, Xiaoyun Wu (systems)

President, The Mailbox Book Company™: Joseph C. Bucci
Director of Book Planning and Development: Chris Poindexter
Book Development Managers: Elizabeth H. Lindsay, Thad McLaurin, Susan Walker
Curriculum Director: Karen P. Shelton
Traffic Manager: Lisa K. Pitts
Librarian: Dorothy C. McKinney
Editorial and Freelance Management: Karen A. Brudnak
Editorial Training: Irving P. Crump
Editorial Assistants: Terrie Head, Hope Rodgers, Jan E. Witcher

Table of Contents

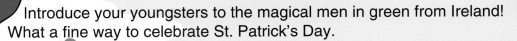

Leapin' Leprechauns!

Introduce your youngsters to the magical men in green from Ireland!
What a fine way to celebrate St. Patrick's Day.

ideas contributed by Stephanie Counce and Ada Hanley Goren

What Is a *Leprechaun?* 💻
Establishing background knowledge

Prepare for this introductory activity by duplicating the leprechaun pattern on page 8 onto tagboard. Cut out the leprechaun and use markers, green and gold glitter, or even metallic confetti to decorate the cutout. Laminate the finished leprechaun for durability, if desired. Then gather your youngsters and introduce them to the Irish legend of the leprechaun.

- Leprechauns were fairies, so they were very tiny and hard to find.

- Leprechauns were the shoemakers for the other fairies. Irish fairies loved to dance, so they were always wearing out their shoes!

- Every leprechaun supposedly kept a pot of gold hidden at the end of the rainbow.

- We often see pictures of leprechauns around St. Patrick's Day.

After sharing some leprechaun lore, invite children to play a game of Find the Leprechaun. Ask a child to hide her eyes while you hide the leprechaun cutout somewhere in the classroom. Then invite the child to open her eyes and begin looking for the hidden leprechaun. Encourage her to ask questions to help her locate the leprechaun—questions which the other students may answer. Or allow the other students to tell the searcher whether she is "hot" (close) or "cold" (far away) in relation to the hiding spot. After she has found the leprechaun, she may hide it for another student to find. Continue until every child has had a turn to search for the hidden leprechaun.

Leprechauns in Literature

Familiarize your students further with leprechauns by reading one or more of the stories from this list.

Clever Tom and the Leprechaun
Written by Linda Shute

Tim O'Toole and the Wee Folk
Written by Gerald McDermott

Catch a Leprechaun
Reciting a song, developing gross-motor skills

Legend has it that if a human can catch a leprechaun, he might just be able to get hold of the leprechaun's pot of gold. With this fun variation of the game Duck, Duck, Goose, your youngsters may get their hands on some gold, too! To prepare for the game, purchase a supply of gold foil-wrapped chocolate coins. Then create a simple leprechaun headband by attaching two pointy green ear shapes to a sentence strip and stapling the strip's ends together so that the headband will fit your students.

To play the game, have students sit in a circle. Place the chocolate coins in a bowl in the center. Designate one child to be the first leprechaun and have him put on the headband. Then have everyone sing the following song as the leprechaun walks around the outside of the circle. Instruct the leprechaun to tap each child as he walks past. On the word "gold," the child who is tapped jumps up and chases the leprechaun around the circle. If the leprechaun successfully reaches the tapped child's empty seat without being tagged, the pursuer puts on the headband and becomes the next leprechaun—repeating the song and the chase. If the tapped child catches (tags) the leprechaun, he not only becomes the next leprechaun, but he also receives a chocolate coin from the bowl and the caught leprechaun must sit in the center to "guard the gold" until another leprechaun is caught. At the conclusion of the game, give all your players a chocolate coin for being good sports!

(sung to the tune of "Mary Had a Little Lamb")

A leprechaun lives in the woods,
In the woods, in the woods.
I would catch him if I could,
To get his pot of gold.

Hidden Gold
Using the sense of touch, counting and comparing sets

This activity will have your little ones searching for the leprechaun's hidden gold in your sensory table. To prepare, color ten or more pounds of uncooked rice green. For each pound of rice, mix together 1/4 cup of rubbing alcohol and a few drops of green food coloring. Pour the rice and the alcohol mixture into a quart-size resealable plastic bag. Shake the bag until the rice is well coated; then pour the colored rice onto sheets of newspaper to dry overnight. Also, in advance, collect some plastic checkers or cut some disks from cardboard. Spray-paint the checkers or disks gold, and allow those to dry overnight as well. Finally, prepare a pot for each child by stapling a pipe cleaner handle to a paper cup.

Pour all the green rice into your sensory table. Then bury the gold coins in the simulated grass. Give each child in a small group a pot labeled with her name. Invite the children to dig through the grass to find the gold coins, placing the coins in their pots as they go. When all the coins have been found, invite each child to count her coins. Compare the quantities found, using terms such as *more, fewer, most,* and *fewest.* Then ask the children to bury the coins for the next group to find and count.

Matthew

Leprechaun Finger Puppets 🖥
Developing fine-motor skills

Your youngsters will be dancing for joy when they make these cute finger puppets! For each child, duplicate one of the finger puppet patterns on page 8. Have each child color his leprechaun, preferably with green clothes. Have him cut around the outline; then assist him as necessary in cutting out the holes on the dotted lines. To make the puppet move, direct the child to place the index and middle fingers of one hand through the holes to simulate the leprechaun's legs. Encourage your little ones to make their puppets walk, run, or dance an Irish jig! They may want to use their puppets to accompany the singing of the following song:

I'm a Little Leprechaun
(sung to the tune of "I'm a Little Teapot")

I'm a little leprechaun.
My clothes are green.
I live by myself—
Don't like to be seen.
If you want my gold,
You can hunt for me,
But I'm as tricky as I can be!

Kick Up Your Heels
Participating in creative movement

Do your little ones love to dance as much as the Irish fairies do? Give them a chance to move to some Irish music in honor of St. Patrick's Day. Perhaps one of your students' parents or another adult in your community could visit the classroom to demonstrate an Irish jig. If that's not possible, locate some music with an Irish flair (such as that by the Chieftains or James Galway) and invite youngsters to move as they please! Add to the fun by supplying each youngster with a green crepe paper streamer to swirl in the air. You'll have a room full of leapin' lads and lassies!

St. Patrick's Day Snacks

Celebrate St. Patrick's Day with some treats that are just right for your little leprechauns. Make Magical Leprechaun Liquid for some science lessons disguised as fun!

Magical Leprechaun Liquid
Communicating observations

A special present from a leprechaun will be the hit of snacktime! In advance, purchase a package of lemonade-flavored Kool-Aid® drink mix, and bring in a bottle of blue food coloring and some sugar. Pour the contents of the envelope and one cup of sugar into a resealable plastic bag. With a permanent marker, write "Magic Powder" on the bag. Write "Magic Potion" on a piece of masking tape. Wrap the tape around the bottle of blue food coloring. On an index card, write the following directions:

1. Pour the Magic Powder into a pitcher. Add 2 quarts of cold water.
2. Pour some of this drink into your cup.
3. Squeeze in one drop of Magic Potion. Stir. Surprise!

On the chalkboard, write a note similar to the one shown. When students find the note, the ingredients, and the directions, they'll be anxious to make this treat! As students watch, mix up the Kool-Aid®, following the directions. (To enhance the yellow color of the Kool-Aid® and make a brighter green later, squeeze several drops of yellow food coloring into the pitcher before mixing the Kool-Aid®.) Give each child a plastic spoon and a clear plastic cup of Kool-Aid®. Carefully add one drop of the blue food coloring into each child's cup and have her stir it in. Then listen for the "Wow!" as students watch their drinks turn green.

Hi, boys and girls!
    I hear you've been learning all about leprechauns! Here are the ingredients to make my favorite drink. It's called Magical Leprechaun Liquid. Follow the directions with your teacher. I hope you like it! Happy St. Patrick's Day!

Love,
Lucky the Leprechaun

Magic Potion

Magic Powder

Leprechaun Lollipops
Discovering properties of matter

Prepare another batch of Magical Leprechaun Liquid. Point out to your students that the drink is a *liquid*—which means it can be poured and it takes the shape of whatever container it is placed in. Demonstrate this by pouring the drink into two or three different clear containers as students watch. Then tell the children that this magical drink can change into a *solid*—a form that has its own shape and that can't be poured. Pour the drink into several ice-cube trays and take them to a freezer. After an hour or two, have an adult volunteer place half of a craft stick into each compartment of the trays. Then let the mixture freeze until solid (about four more hours). Show children the trays. Attempt to pour the cubes out. Discuss how the liquid has changed. Then pop out the treats and invite youngsters to enjoy this new treat—Leprechaun Lollipops!

Leprechaun Finger Puppets
Use with "Leprechaun Finger Puppets" on page 6.

Leprechaun Pattern
Use with "What Is a *Leprechaun?*" on page 4.

Shamrock Showcase

Share the splendor of shamrocks with your students in this thematic unit that will have everyone feeling lucky!

ideas contributed by Janet Czapla and Ada Hanley Goren

The Search Is On
Recognizing similarities and differences in plants

Begin your study of shamrocks by sending your students on a search for a bit of luck. Bring in a real shamrock plant (or a picture of one) for students to examine. Point out the three leaflets on the plant. Tell students that the shamrock is the national symbol of Ireland. Clover—which grows in the United States—is similar. Take your class outside and help them locate patches of clover. As children are collecting clover, challenge them to find a lucky four-leaf clover. While your students are searching, have another teacher or an assistant place a precut four-leaf clover at each child's seat or cubby. When your youngsters return to the classroom, they will be thrilled to find a lucky clover of their own! As a follow-up activity, place the shamrock plant (or picture) and the gathered clover in your science area for students to observe.

Shamrock Attire
Developing fine-motor skills

Celebrate the Emerald Isle with these nifty neckties! Make several nine-inch, tie-shaped patterns out of tagboard. Provide each child with a piece of light green construction paper and several 1 1/2-inch dark green shamrock cutouts. Have each student trace a tie pattern on his light green paper. After students cut out their ties, help each child fold down the top 1 1/2 inches of his tie and staple it to form a flap. Then have each youngster glue his shamrock cutouts on the front of his tie. To complete the ties, help each student thread yarn or elastic thread through the stapled flap and tie it around his neck. What a dapper bunch of lucky youngsters you have!

The Shape of Shamrocks

Describing observations, demonstrating creativity

Remove your shamrock plant or picture from the science area and display it for all to see. Ask your little ones to describe what it looks like. ("How many leaves does it have? What color is it? What shape are the leaves?") Lead your youngsters to the discovery that each leaf resembles a heart.

After sharing this information, invite students to create individual shamrocks. Demonstrate how to fold a square of green construction paper and cut out a heart as shown. Supply each child with three four-inch green construction paper squares, one 1" x 5" green construction paper strip, and one 9" x 12" sheet of white paper. Have each child glue the strip to the white paper to create a stem. Help each child cut out three hearts and glue the tips together on the strip as shown. Encourage students to use a variety of green materials to decorate their shamrocks, such as green tissue paper, crepe paper, or construction paper; green paint and crayons; glue mixed with green food coloring; green packing peanuts; green pasta pieces; and green shamrock cutouts. When the shamrocks are dry, display them on the bulletin board described in "A Showcase of Shamrocks."

A Showcase of Shamrocks

Repeating a pattern

Your lucky little ones can share their creative talents on this shamrock-filled, student-made display. Cover a bulletin board with yellow bulletin board paper. Mount students' shamrocks from "The Shape of Shamrocks" activity and add the caption "A Showcase of Shamrocks."

Then enlist your youngsters' help in creating a sponge-painted shamrock border. Begin by cutting sponges into three different-sized shamrock shapes. Give each child a strip of adding-machine tape or a 2 1/2-inch-wide strip of white paper. Sponge-paint a shamrock pattern for each student to copy on his strip of paper. When the paint is dry, mount the paper strips around the bulletin board as a border. What better way to showcase your students' splendid shamrocks?

A Showcase of Shamrocks

Ten Green Shamrocks

Demonstrating listening skills, counting backward from 10

Practice the skill of counting backward with this fun rhyming poem. To begin, cut ten shamrocks from green construction paper; then laminate them for durability. Ask children to sit in a circle; then place the shamrocks in the middle. As you recite the following poem, insert a student's name in each blank. When a youngster hears his name, he takes a shamrock from the middle of the circle. When you finish reciting the poem, have students return the shamrocks to the middle of the circle. Begin the poem again, inserting different names in the blanks. Be on the lookout for little ones chiming in during the rhyming parts of the poem.

Ten green shamrocks, oh so fine.
_____ took one; then there were nine.

Nine green shamrocks, growing by the gate.
_____ took one; then there were eight.

Eight green shamrocks, looking up to heaven.
_____ took one; then there were seven.

Seven green shamrocks, straight like sticks.
_____ took one; then there were six.

Six green shamrocks, growing by a hive.
_____ took one; then there were five.

Five green shamrocks, lying on the floor.
_____ took one; then there were four.

Four green shamrocks, you and I can see.
_____ took one; then there were three.

Three green shamrocks, oh so few.
_____ took one; then there were two.

Two green shamrocks, counting them is fun.
_____ took one; then there was one.

One green shamrock, resting in the sun.
_____ took one; now the game is done.

Pass the Shamrock

Developing language and listening skills

Remind your students that many people believe that finding a four-leaf clover is good luck. Invite your little ones to test their luck in this passing game. To prepare, obtain some Irish music, cut out and laminate a four-leaf clover, and make a lucky four-leaf-clover headband. Ask students to sit in a circle and give the clover to one student to hold. Start the music and ask students to pass the four-leaf clover around the circle. After about 20 seconds, stop the music. Whoever is holding the four-leaf clover is the lucky youngster. Invite her to wear the headband and share a time when she has felt lucky. Begin the music again and have the designated lucky person start the passing of the four-leaf clover. Continue until your classroom is filled with lucky learners!

Shamrock Concentration

Increasing visual memory

Students will need both luck and a good memory for this activity! Duplicate the gameboard on page 13 for every two students. Divide students into pairs and have each pair work together to color the shamrocks on their gameboard green. Distribute milk-bottle caps or chips and have students cover all the shamrocks on their boards. Have each pair of students take turns lifting two chips at a time to try to locate matching shamrocks. If a student finds a match, she takes the chips and another turn. If the pictures do not match, the student must cover the shamrocks and wait for her next turn. Play continues until the board is clear. The child in each pair with more chips is the winner.

Shamrock Shuffle

Identifying letters and numbers

You'll get an enthusiastic response to this small-group activity that reinforces letter and number identification skills. Program ten shamrock cutouts with letters or numbers and one shamrock cutout with a smiley face. Place the cutouts in a coffee can covered in green construction paper. Ask students to sit in a circle. To play the game, pass the can around the circle and have the first child draw out a shamrock. If the student draws a shamrock with a letter or a number, he identifies it and puts it back in the can. If the student draws the shamrock with the smiley face, everyone gets up and does the "Shamrock Shuffle" (shuffles to a new spot in the circle). Continue to pass the can around until all students have had a chance to draw from the can. Happy shuffling!

Scrumptious Shamrocks

Following directions, developing fine-motor skills

The shamrock plant might not grow in the United States, but that doesn't mean your students can't have their own shamrocks. Entice your little ones to make this tempting shamrock snack!

To make approximately 30 shamrock-shaped cookies, purchase two rolls of refrigerated sugar-cookie dough. Have each child wash his hands; then give him a 3/8-inch slice of dough and a piece of waxed paper. Help the child divide his slice of dough into four pieces. Have each child roll three pieces of dough into balls and place them together on the waxed paper to form a shamrock. Have the child slightly flatten the balls. Have him roll the extra piece of dough into a snake to form a stem as shown. Encourage the student to cover his shamrock cookie with green sugar sprinkles. Place the cookies on a foil-lined cookie sheet. Use a permanent marker to write each child's name on the foil beside his cookie. Bake the cookies according to the directions provided on the cookie-dough wrapper. Cool the cookies on baking sheets before serving them.

Reach for a Rainbow!

Invite your young scientists to investigate one of nature's most colorful gifts…the rainbow.

ideas contributed by Suzanne Moore

Getting Ready ⌨

Before you begin your study of rainbows, duplicate a class quantity of Parent Note 1 on page 20. It lists many of the items you'll need for your youngsters to complete the hands-on experiences described in this unit. On each child's copy, check off the item(s) you'd like his family to send to school; then send the note home.

Rainbow Realities
Building prior knowledge

On the first day of your rainbow unit, display a photograph or an illustration of a rainbow. Ask your youngsters if any of them have seen a real rainbow. When did they see it? After giving children a chance to share what they already know about rainbows, share these intriguing facts:

What is a rainbow?

A rainbow is made of light. Sunlight looks colorless to our eyes, but it really contains lots of colors! We see those colors when the sun's rays pass through drops of rain. The water bends and separates the light into its many colors—a rainbow!

Actually rainbows *are* formed every time it rains; but for us to see a rainbow, all the angles must be just right between the sun, the raindrops, and our eyes. Sometimes the sun is too high or too low in the sky, or we are facing the wrong direction in relation to the sun.

What colors are in a rainbow?

The colors of a rainbow always appear in the same sequence from top to bottom: red, orange, yellow, green, blue, purple.

What shape is a rainbow?

A rainbow is really a circle. The horizon obstructs our view of the other half of the circle, so what we see is an arc.

Your little artists will no doubt be anxious to illustrate some rainbows, so let the drawing begin! As children are working, circulate throughout the room and ask each child to tell you something he has learned about rainbows. Write his dictation below his picture.

Let's Make Rainbows!

Describing observations in detail

There are a number of ways you and your students can create rainbowlike bands of colors. Try one or more of the following experiments. Provide time for students to describe their observations in detail.

- On a sunny day, place a large fishbowl or another clear container of water on a windowsill. When the sunlight hits the bowl at the proper angle, a rainbow will form on the surface opposite the sun. If the sun is not shining, try shining a flashlight from various angles to achieve this effect.

- If you have prisms available at your school or center, give one to each child in a small group. Provide a sunny location or flashlights, and encourage the children to use the prisms to produce their own rainbows.

- Take the science lesson outside on a warm spring day! In advance, make a bubble solution using the provided recipe. Invite youngsters to make bubble blowers from pipe cleaners. On a sunny day, give each child a plastic cup of bubble solution; then challenge him to look for the rainbow on each bubble he blows.

   If you can't go outside, pour some bubble solution into an individual foil tart pan for each child. Have each child use a straw to blow bubbles in his solution. (Caution children NOT to suck on the straws.) Once the top of each child's pan is covered with bubbles, provide him with a hand lens to observe the bubbles closely. Ask if he can see the rainbows. If you don't have enough natural light in your classroom, try shining a flashlight on the bubbles from different angles.

Bubble Solution

1 gal. water
2/3 c. Joy® or Dawn® dishwashing liquid
1 tbsp. glycerin

For the best results, allow this mixture to sit for at least five days.

A Rainbow Line
Reinforcing the order of color in a rainbow

Reinforce the order of the colors in a rainbow with this fun way to line up. Divide your class into six groups. Assign a color to each group, and give each child in the group a yarn necklace in the group's assigned color. Each time students line up, choose a leader from the red group. The leader may choose a child to be next in line—as long as the chosen child is wearing an orange necklace! Instruct the second child to choose someone wearing a yellow necklace, and so forth, following the order of a rainbow's colors until every child is in line. How many complete rainbows can your class make?

Rainbow Scavenger Hunt 🖥
Sorting by color

Prepare a table in your classroom to serve as the Rainbow Sorting Center. Cut strips of red, orange, yellow, green, blue, and purple bulletin board paper in equal widths. Tape these in order on a long table. Then duplicate Parent Note 2 on page 20 for each child. Give each child a copy of the note and a gallon-sized, resealable plastic bag to take home. When a student brings in his collection of colored items, have him sort each item onto the corresponding color strip at the Rainbow Sorting Center. Provide a box or basket at the center where items can be placed when the center is not in use or when you want to scramble the items to be re-sorted.

Make a Rainbow

Rainbow Roll 🖥
Identifying color words

This colorful game will emphasize the color sequence of a rainbow and help little ones practice color-word recognition, too! To prepare the game, first convert an empty tissue box into a large color cube. Wrap the box (gift-wrapped style) in white or black bulletin board paper. Then glue a circle cut from a different color of construction paper—red, orange, yellow, green, blue, or purple—onto each of the cube's six sides. If desired, cover the cube with clear Con-Tact® paper for durability.

Next, make four copies of the gameboard on page 21 on tagboard and laminate them. Provide four sets of yarn pieces (cut to the lengths listed below). Give one set of yarn pieces to each group of two to four players. To play the game, each player takes a turn rolling the color cube. The color on top of the cube indicates which color of yarn the player is to place on her gameboard. If she rolls a color she has already placed on her rainbow, play goes to the next player. As each player completes her rainbow, reward her with a snack-size treat of Skittles® candies!

Yarn Lengths

red—13 inches
orange—11 inches
yellow—9 inches
green—7 inches
blue—5 inches
purple—3 1/2 inches

Yarn Lengths

red—7 inches
orange—5 1/2 inches
yellow—5 inches
green—4 inches
blue—3 inches
purple—2 1/2 inches

Magnetic Rainbow
Reinforcing the colors of a rainbow, developing fine-motor skills

These beautiful magnets will attract lots of attention! Provide a three- to four-inch plastic lid for each child (lids from eight-ounce containers of margarine, sour cream, or ricotta cheese work well). Use a permanent marker to write each child's name on the outside (top) of his lid before beginning. Invite each student to paint the inside of his lid with thick blue tempera paint. After the paint dries, provide each child with six lengths of thick yarn in the colors and lengths listed above. Ask each youngster to glue the lengths of yarn onto the blue paint in sequence to form a rainbow. Give each child two cotton balls. Show him how to pull the cotton balls apart slightly to spread them out; then have him glue the cotton below his yarn rainbow to represent clouds. Add a strip of magnetic tape to the back of each project before sending it home to add some rainbow razzle-dazzle to the family's refrigerator!

Color Weaving
Representing a rainbow's color sequence, developing fine-motor skills

Encourage youngsters to practice sequencing and fine-motor skills with these wonderful weavings! In advance, prepare a weaving mat for each child by using six twist ties to attach three sets of plastic six-pack rings together, as shown. Working with one small group at a time, provide each youngster with six 12-inch lengths of crepe paper streamers—each length a different rainbow color. Demonstrate how to weave the crepe paper streamers in and out of the holes in the six-pack rings. Have each child begin with the red streamer at the top of his mat and follow the color order of a rainbow, ending with the purple streamer at the bottom. When each child's project is finished, tie one end of a 12-inch length of yarn to each of the top corners. Display these wall hangings in your classroom or send them home for youngsters to share with their families.

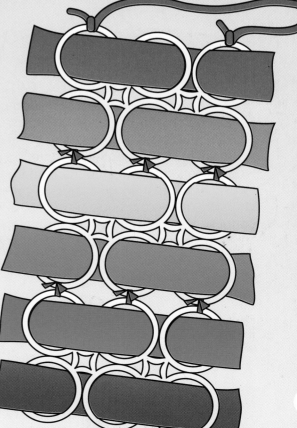

"Rainbow Salad" Booklet
Creating illustrations to match text

Your youngsters will be raiding their refrigerators for rainbow colors after completing this delicious booklet! In advance, decide how you would like the children to illustrate their booklets. If you want them to make fingerprints to represent some or all of the fruits, provide either an ink pad or a shallow dish of tempera paint in each color needed. Or have the children tear and crumple pieces of colored tissue paper, or cut out likenesses of the fruits from construction paper to glue on their pages.

Copy the booklet on pages 22 and 23 for each child. Assist each child in cutting apart her pages, sequencing them, and stapling them together at the left. Have each student write her name on the booklet cover and use crayons to color the rainbow on the cover and the bowl's stripes on pages 1–6. Then have each child illustrate her booklet with your chosen medium. Encourage the children to "read" their finished booklets to one another and to their families to reinforce their recognition of color words!

Rainbow Salad

by

Stephen Doughty

Rainbow salad!

7

A Real Rainbow Salad
Showing an understanding of text

Of course, the perfect way to follow up the " 'Rainbow Salad' Booklet" is to make a *real* rainbow salad. Ask parents to donate the appropriate ingredients (use frozen or canned fruits for those which aren't in season), and invite youngsters to help you follow the booklet "recipe" to create a colorful snacktime treat! While students are enjoying cups of rainbow salad, play a recording of one of these "Rainbow Tunes."

Rainbow Tunes

"The World Is a Rainbow"
Sung by Greg & Steve
We All Live Together—Volume 2

"I Know the Colors in the Rainbow"
Sung by Fred Koch
Did You Feed My Cow?

"Rainbow of Colors"
Sung by Greg & Steve
We All Live Together—Volume 5

Read About Rainbows

Your youngsters will enjoy these rainbow-related literature selections and the accompanying activities.

I would climb it.

A Rainbow of My Own
by Don Freeman
Making a personal connection

This is the story of a young boy's experiences with an imaginary rainbow playmate. After reading it aloud, ask your students what kinds of games they would play if they had rainbows of *their* own. Give each child half of a flattened nine-inch paper plate. Ask her to draw a rainbow on her half plate; then have her glue her rainbow to a sheet of 12" x 18" construction paper and illustrate her idea for playing with a rainbow. Write each child's dictation on her page; then bind the pages together between construction paper covers. Write the title "If I Could Play With a Rainbow,…" on the front cover. Add the book to your reading center for students to enjoy.

More Rainbow Reading

Planting a Rainbow
by Lois Ehlert

The Rainbow Fish
Written by Marcus Pfister

Rain
Written by Robert Kalan

Rainbow Crow
retold by Nancy Van Laan
Making and describing observations

The text is a bit long in this traditional Lenape legend, but with some paraphrasing and explanation, youngsters will enjoy this tale about the heroic Rainbow Crow. Crow lost his bright colors while bringing Fire to Earth; but with careful observation, you and your students can still see rainbow colors hidden in his black feathers.

After reading the story, show your students how to find rainbow colors hidden in black ink. Give each child a 2" x 6" strip of a paper towel stapled to one end of a craft stick, as shown. Have each child use a water-soluble black marker to write his name on his stick and to draw a dot near the unstapled end of the paper-towel strip. Pour a little water into a clear plastic cup for each child. Have each student hold his stick and place his paper-towel strip into his cup, so that the end of the strip just touches the water. Have students carefully observe as the paper towel absorbs the water. When the water reaches the black ink, they will be amazed to see the dyes separate and spread into colorful patterns. Encourage students to describe what they see!

John

Parent Note 1

Use with "Getting Ready" on page 14.

Dear Family,

Our class will begin studying rainbows on _____.
(date)

You can help by sending in any of the materials checked below as soon as possible:

_____ individual foil tart pans
_____ plastic straws
_____ thick yarn (red, orange, yellow, green, blue, or purple)
_____ crepe paper streamers (red, orange, yellow, green, blue, or purple)
_____ plastic six-pack rings
_____ twist ties
_____ plastic lids from 8-oz. containers of margarine, sour cream, or similar products
_____ white cotton balls
_____ other: _____

Thank you for participating in your child's learning!

Parent Note 2

Use with "Rainbow Scavenger Hunt" on page 16.

Rainbow Scavenger Hunt

Dear Family,

We are learning about rainbows at school. Did you know that there are six colors in a rainbow? Please help your child go on a Rainbow Scavenger Hunt at your house. Help your child find one small, nonreturnable item in each color of the rainbow. Place the items in the plastic bag, seal it, and return it to school by _____.
(date)

We'll place all these items in a Rainbow Sorting Center where the children will sort them by color.

Thank you for participating in your child's learning!

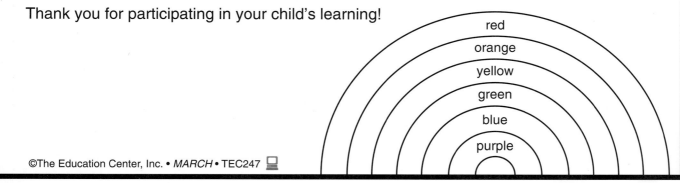

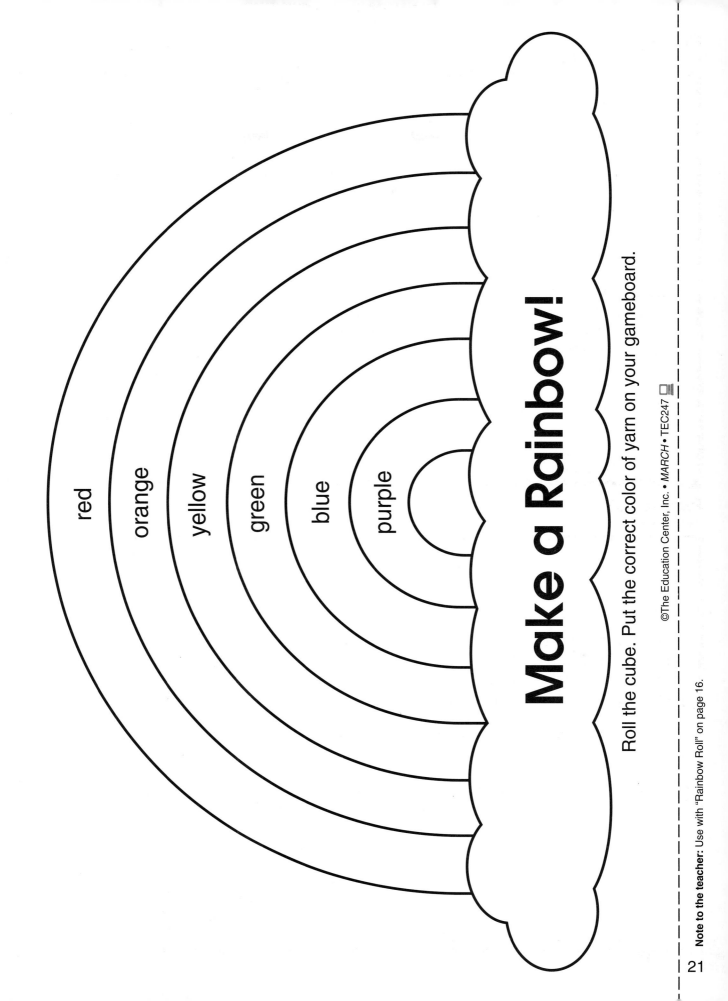

Make a Rainbow!

red

orange

yellow

green

blue

purple

Roll the cube. Put the correct color of yarn on your gameboard.

21

Note to the teacher: Use with "Rainbow Roll" on page 16.

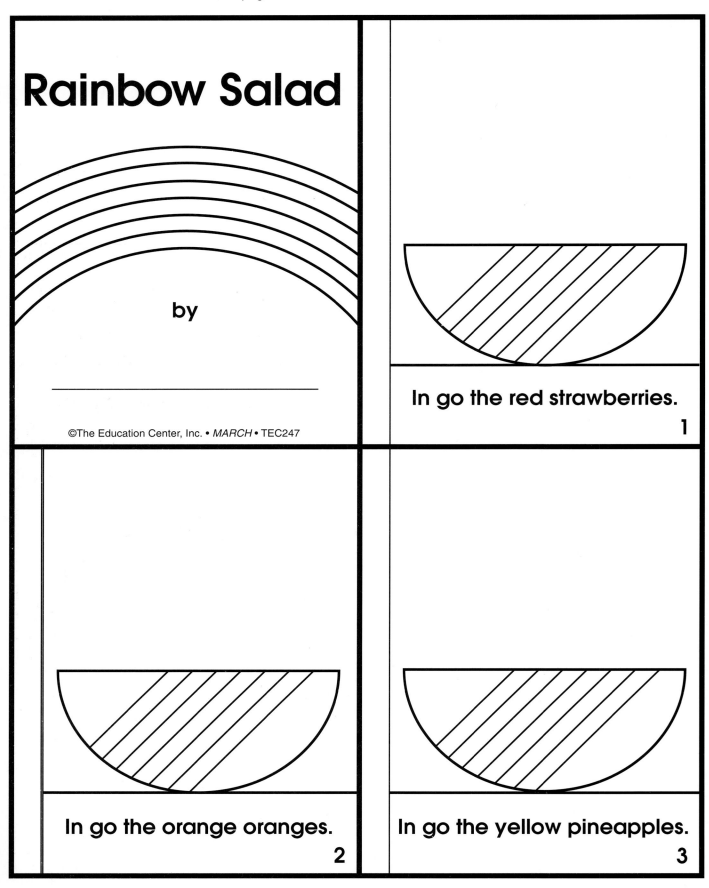

Rainbow Salad

by

_____

In go the red strawberries.

1

In go the orange oranges.

2

In go the yellow pineapples.

3

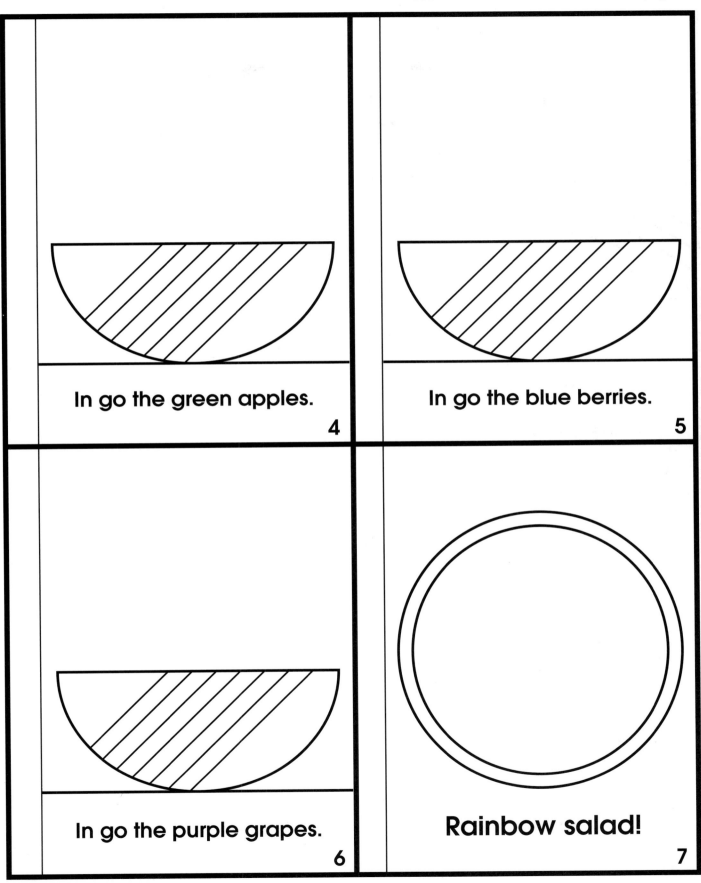

In go the green apples.

4

In go the blue berries.

5

In go the purple grapes.

6

Rainbow salad!

7

HERE COMES SPRING!

Planting, building, cleaning, chirping, growing, wakening...it must be spring! Use the following activities to chase away those winter doldrums and spark an epidemic of spring fever. Your little ones will be amazed at the changes happening all around.

ideas contributed by Barbara Backer and Angie Kutzer

SPRING'S MYSTERIES

Using prior knowledge, making predictions

Introduce your spring unit with this guessing game. To prepare, cover a box with gift wrap or Con-Tact® covering in a springtime print. Put a collection of spring-related objects inside the box, such as a bird's feather, a small blossom, an umbrella, and a pack of seeds. During group time, tell your students that they are going to guess what the next unit of study will be. Have a child come forward and pick one clue from the box. Direct him to show it to the group. Ask for the object's name; then ask if anyone has a guess for the unit's topic. Have another child pick a clue from the box. Question the children again. Repeat this procedure until all of the objects have been chosen and named. End the activity by confirming children's guesses that it's all about spring!

SPRING THINGS

kites
bunnies
robins
flowers
green leaves

SPRING THINGS

Recalling facts from nonfiction

Channel all of the excitement aroused during "Spring's Mysteries" into a fact-gathering session. In advance, cut a large sun shape from bulletin board paper. Read *When Spring Comes* by Robert Maass to your group, and discuss the many characteristics of this season. List these spring words and phrases on the sun cutout along with the title "Spring Things." Keep this list handy so that students can add to it during the rest of the unit.

LOOKING FOR SPRING

Making observations, representing an oral message in writing

Once your little ones have made a good listing of spring things, grab your camera and take your group outdoors to search for signs of spring. Take an instant picture of each child holding or pointing to an item that indicates spring has arrived. Return to the classroom, attach the pictures to a sheet of chart paper, and take dictation about each child's find. Hang this refreshing chart out in the hallway to remind everyone that spring has sprung!

"I found a pretty flower."

Payton

TIME TO PLANT!
Understanding the growth cycle of a plant

Spring means warm, moist soil—perfect for planting! Use the story *Planting a Rainbow* by Lois Ehlert to help your little ones understand a garden's growing cycle. Use the reproducible on page 30 to encourage your students to "plant" their own gardens. Have each child draw what she would like to grow in a garden. Write her completion to the sentence, "I will plant _____ in my garden." Provide real seeds for your children to glue in the "dirt" at the bottoms of their pages. Combine these pictures in a class book titled "Our Gardens." Imaginations are sure to sprout up all kinds of garden goodies!

A CLASS OF GRASS
Observing plant growth

Give your budding gardeners some hands-on experience with plant growth. Divide the number of children in your group in half and obtain that many large, Styrofoam® take-out boxes. Cut on the hinge of each box, separating the lids from the plates. You will also need a bag of potting soil, a few misting bottles, and a bag of grass seed. Distribute a lid or plate to each child. Have him scoop some soil out of the bag and lightly pack it in his tray. Then direct him to sprinkle two or three handfuls of seed over the dirt and to pat the seeds lightly into the soil. Pass around the filled misting bottles so that your little ones can water their seeds.

While waiting for the grass to grow, invite your youngsters to add some interest to their grass gardens. Have each child draw a house on construction paper, tape the house to a craft stick, and place it at the edge of his tray so that the grass will now resemble a front yard. Once the grass has grown quite a bit, give your little ones that spring experience that's not so fun for grown-ups—mowing the lawn! Encourage them to crank up their scissors and start trimming!

Note: Depending on the variety of seed, the grass should sprout in seven to ten days.

"TREE-RIFIC" SPRING
Describing seasonal changes

Explore the area outside your classroom to find a tree that has definite seasonal changes. On the same day each week, lead your children out to observe while you take a picture of the tree. Pin the photo to your classroom calendar and discuss with your youngsters how the tree has changed each week. Take these pictures until the tree completes its spring transformation. After the last discussion, use the photos in a pocket chart for a "tree-mendous" sequencing opportunity!

SCRUB-A-DUB!

Understanding that seasonal changes in weather affect behavior

Spring's warmer weather allows people to spruce up their homes and surroundings after the harshness of winter. Celebrate the new season by having a spring-cleaning day with your youngsters. They will enjoy sweeping sidewalks, scrubbing outside walls with soft brushes, and picking up litter and twigs. On an especially warm spring day, provide sponges and buckets of water for cleaning toy vehicles. Wash away winter and spiff up for spring!

A BUILDING BOOM

Understanding that seasonal changes in weather affect behavior

Construction also swings into high gear during spring's warm weather. Take a walk with your little ones to see if there is any new construction in your area. If so, walk by often to discuss the progress being made and to observe any machinery in action. Bring the skills of building to your class by setting up indoor and outdoor construction centers.

For an outdoor center, provide tools sized correctly for young children, smooth wood scraps, safety goggles, and preschool nails (one inch long with broad, flat heads). Draw spring designs on thick tree-stump pieces for students to trace by hammering nails. Before opening the center, model safety rules and establish a limit to the number of workers at the center at one time. (As always, supervision is the best precaution.)

For an indoor center, provide containers of pretzel sticks, gum-drops, large marshmallows, Gummy candies, and caramel cubes. Encourage your little ones to construct a few edible edifices. Hard hats are desired, but not required!

MANUFACTURING MELODY 🖥

Reciting and dramatizing a song

Teach your little ones the following song to sing as they panto-mime motions or build structures at the centers described in "A Building Boom":

BUILDING A NEW HOUSE!
(sung to the tune of "Jimmy Crack Corn")

Look at them hit and pound the nails.
Look at them tote the cement pails.
Look at them paint the tall porch rails.
They're building a new house!

ROOSTS FOR ROBINS
Observing the behavior of birds

That first robin is always a sight for winter-worn eyes! Show your little ones a picture of the male robin (with his red breast) and explain that these birds are among the first to return north in the spring. Robins also are known to return to the same areas each year to build their nests. They typically use roots, grass stems, twigs, rags, string, and paper for nest building. Promote the robins' return to your area by having your children collect materials that a robin could use in her nest. (Females usually do the building.) Instruct your students to hang these on a fence, then watch to see what is chosen. They might even hear, "Cheerily cheery"—the robins' song—as a thank-you.

NUTTY NESTS
Following directions

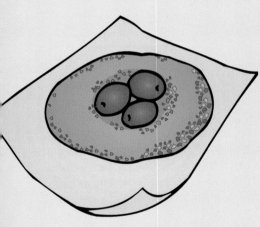

Entice your little spring birds with this delicious nest-building experience. Prepare the nut mixture using the recipe shown. To make a nest, have each child take a spoonful of nut mixture and roll it into a ball. Have her place the ball on waxed paper and flatten it slightly with the palm of her hand. Show her how to use her thumb to make a deep print in the middle of the nest. Provide small grapes to serve as eggs. Beware—your little ones may start chirping for more!

NUT MIXTURE
(makes nine three-inch nests)

1 c. nut topping
(finely chopped nuts)
1/2 c. peanut butter
3 tbsp. flour

Mix all ingredients with a spoon until well blended.

WHO'S MY PARENT? 💻
Matching animal offspring and their parents

As spring emerges, so do many baby animals. Use the animal cards on page 31 to prepare a matching game that's budding with new babies. First duplicate page 32 for later use. Then cut apart and laminate the cards on page 31. Attach the parent cards to one cube-shaped gift box; attach the baby cards to another cube-shaped gift box. Have one child roll both cubes. Ask the child if the parent and baby showing on the tops of the cubes go together. If they do, encourage the whole class to make that animal's sound. If the parent and baby do not go together, have everyone snap their fingers once. Continue until each child has had a turn to roll the cubes.

SPRINGTIME READING AREA

Promoting an interest in reading

Set the mood for your blossoming bookworms with this outdoor reading center. Spread a couple of blankets on the ground and furnish picnic baskets full of springtime stories from the list below.

STORIES FOR SPRING FEVER

The Boy Who Didn't Believe in Spring
Written by Lucille Clifton

Hopper Hunts for Spring
Written by Marcus Pfister

My Spring Robin
Written by Anne Rockwell

Rabbit's Good News
Written by Ruth Lercher Bornstein

That's What Happens When It's Spring!
Written by Elaine W. Good

The Spring Rabbit
Written by Joyce Dunbar

SPRING INTO ACTION

Identifying action words

Create this dynamic bulletin board display using your youngsters' illustrations. Cover a board with strips of red, orange, yellow, green, blue, and purple bulletin board paper. Title the board "Spring Into Action" with black lettering. Review with your children the class list from the "Spring Things" activity on page 24; then discuss what actions each of the objects or animals listed performs. Instruct each child to illustrate a different action word. Have your children share their drawings with their class-mates. Then jump, hop, and run over to attach the pictures to your board!

COUNTING ON A COLORFUL SPRING

Identifying colors and color words, following oral directions

Reinforce number and color concepts with your little ones by having them color and count their way through this spring booklet. For each child, duplicate pages 32 and 33, and provide the following materials: scissors, crayons, one piece of blue plastic wrap, two yellow mini muffin liners, glitter (optional), three orange kites cut from felt, four seven-millimeter wiggle eyes, five small white pom-poms, six purple sequins or beads, glue, access to a red ink pad and a fine black marker, and a length of narrow green ribbon (approximately 20 inches).

Help each child cut apart her booklet pages. Guide your students to complete each page as described. When each youngster's pages are dry, assemble and staple them on the left side between construction paper covers. Instruct each child to draw a spring scene on the front of her booklet. Title the booklet "It Must Be Spring!"

Page 1: Use a blue crayon to color the word *blue.* Glue the piece of blue plastic wrap to the top of the page.

Page 2: Use a yellow crayon to color the word *yellow.* Flatten two yellow mini muffin liners and glue them to the page. Spread glue on the liners and sprinkle them with glitter if desired.

Page 3: Use an orange crayon to color the word *orange.* Color the kite tails. Glue a kite-shaped cutout to the top of each kite string.

Page 4: Use a brown crayon to color the word *brown* and to color the frogs. Glue a seven-millimeter wiggle eye on each frog.

Page 5: Glue a small white pom-pom to the X on each bunny.

Page 6: Use a purple crayon to color the word *purple.* Color the stems and leaves green. Glue a purple bead or sequin to the top of each stem.

Page 7: Use a red crayon to color the word *red.* Press one finger onto the red stamp pad; then make seven fingerprints on the page. Add black dots, details, and legs with the marker.

Page 8: Use a green crayon to color the word *green.* Cut the length of green ribbon into eight pieces; then glue the pieces to the page.

One blue sky.

Two yellow suns.

Three orange kites.

Four brown peepers.

Five white bunnies.

Six purple flowers.

Seven red ladybugs.

Eight green grass blades.

Name _____

I will plant _____

_____ in my garden.

Note to the teacher: Use with "Time to Plant!" on page 25.

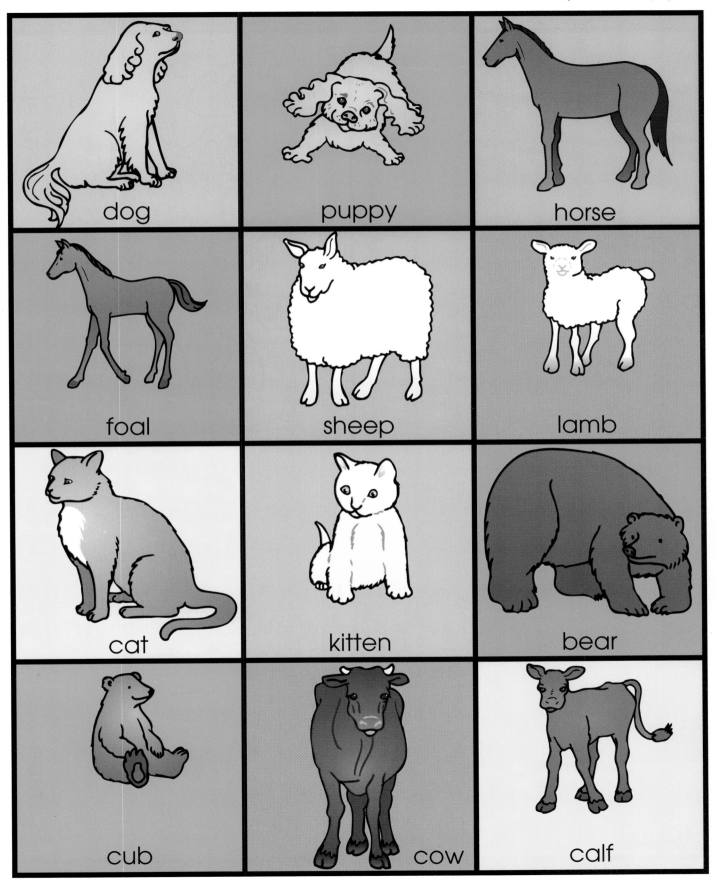

dog

puppy

horse

foal

sheep

lamb

cat

kitten

bear

cub

cow

calf

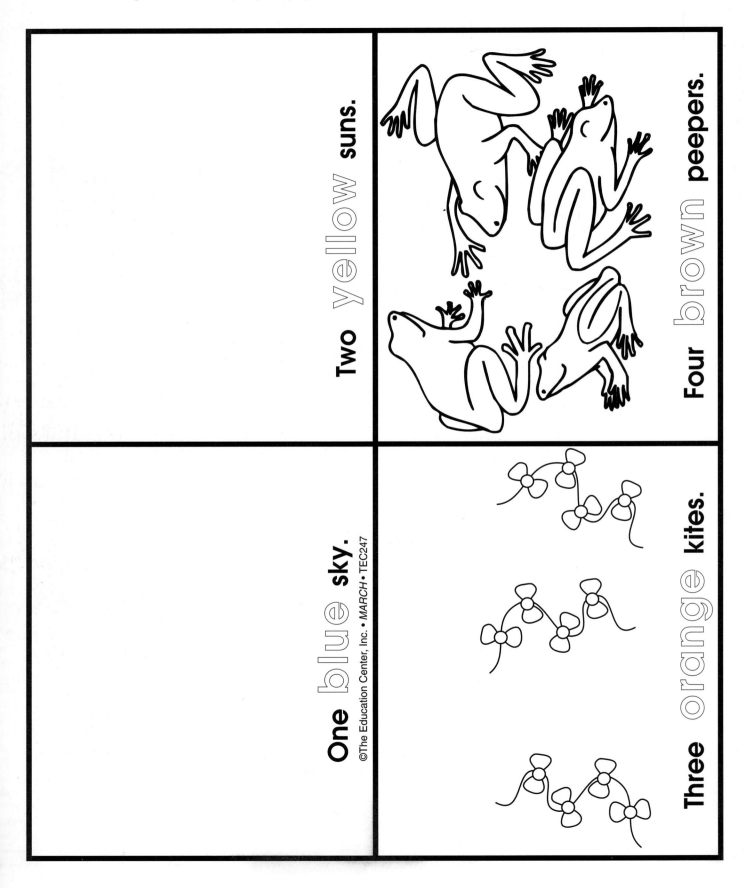

Two yellow suns.

Four brown peepers.

One blue sky.

©The Education Center, Inc. • *MARCH* • TEC247

Three orange kites.

Six purple flowers.

Eight green blades of grass.

Five white bunnies.

Seven red ladybugs.

When the Wind Blows...

Whether it's a hurricane or a gentle puff, wind is pretty interesting stuff! Teach your little learners about wind with these uplifting activities.

ideas contributed by Lucia Kemp Henry

What About Wind?

Building on prior knowledge

Begin your wind unit by reading the amusing story *The Wind Blew* by Pat Hutchins. After sharing this tale of the wind whisking away a variety of objects, ask youngsters to tell about their experiences with the wind. Has anyone ever lost anything in the wind—as the characters in the story did? Has anyone ever been frightened by the wind? After giving each youngster a chance to contribute to the conversation, share some facts about the wind:

- Wind is moving air.
- We can't see wind, but we can sometimes hear it and see its effects, such as when it moves tree branches or causes ripples in water.
- Some winds blow gently; others blow fiercely. In a hurricane, winds can blow more than 100 miles an hour—about twice as fast as cars on a highway!
- People use wind to help them move things, such as kites and sailboats.
- The wind blows clouds from place to place, so changes in the wind often mean changes in the weather.

Wind Watchers

Making and stating observations

On a breezy day, invite your little ones to do a little wind watching. Take the class outside and have them look for signs of the wind. Take along a clipboard and make notes of the things students see. Or—better yet—take along a video camera and record the wind's effects. Remind students to look for movements in plants and objects, such as swaying grass or tree branches, a swinging sign, someone's hair or jacket blowing in a breeze, or even the movement of clouds overhead. Once you've returned to the classroom, encourage youngsters to help you record their observations on a sheet of chart paper. Title your experience story "Watching the Wind." Ask a few student volunteers to illustrate some of the observations in the margins of the chart paper. Then display the story on a classroom wall throughout your study of the wind.

Watching the Wind
by Mrs. Jerrett's Class
Leaves were blowing on the trees. The grass moved a little bit. The wind blew Danielle's hair. Mrs. Jerrett's skirt was blowing, too!

A Windy Experiment

Recognizing the effects of wind

Draft your little scientists to conduct an experiment on what the wind will blow—and what it won't. Bring in a child-safe electric fan (with a cage around the blades) and provide plenty of supervision. Set the fan on a tabletop, along with items from the list below.

drinking straw	aluminum foil scrap
cardboard scrap	leaf
cotton ball	paper clip
crayon	a construction paper scrap
pencil eraser	plastic spoon
seashell	small rock
feather	

Also prepare two classification mats. Cut a large sheet of poster board in half. Label one half "yes" and the other half "no." Print the question "Will the Wind Blow It?" on a sentence strip, and place the title strip and poster board mats on another table.

When all is ready, ask youngsters to imagine that the air blowing from the fan is the wind. Ask a volunteer to pick up one of the objects and hold it in front of the fan and then let go. If the fan's breeze blows the object, ask the volunteer to place it on the poster board labeled "yes." If the object falls onto the tabletop, ask the volunteer to place it on the poster board labeled "no." Continue until all the objects have been tested. Leave the objects on display for reference throughout your unit.

A Song About the Wind

Applying learned knowledge, reciting a song 💻

Teach youngsters this simple song about the wind. Sing the chorus and verse once for the children; then have youngsters brainstorm a list of words to insert into the verse, based on their findings in "Wind Watchers" (page 34) and "A Windy Experiment." Write the list on chart paper and add a small drawing next to each word on the list as a visual reminder. Then sing the song together as many times as desired, each time letting a different child choose a word to insert in the verse.

The Wind Can Blow
(sung to the tune of "The Farmer in the Dell")

Chorus:
The wind can blow, blow, blow.
The wind can blow, blow, blow.
Oh-ho, now do you know?
The wind can blow, blow, blow.

Verse:
The wind can blow [a tree].
The wind can blow [a tree].
Oh-ho, now do you know?
The wind can blow [a tree].

Windy Poetry

Reciting a song, demonstrating listening skills 🖥️

Poetry is a breeze with activities like these! Use the picture cards on page 41 to make visual prompts for this poem or to create a pocket-chart reading activity. Duplicate the picture cards on page 41 on tagboard. Color the pictures; then laminate them for durability, if desired. Distribute a card to each of 12 students. As the class recites each line of the poem, have the student with the corresponding picture hold up his card.

For a variation, print each line of the poem on a separate sentence strip, omitting the boldfaced words. Insert the strips into a pocket chart and add the picture cards in the appropriate spaces to make a rebus reading activity.

The wind blows high in the top of the **tree.**
The wind blows the **grass** down low.
The wind blows the **leaves** in a swirling whirl.
The wind makes the **sailboat** go.

The wind blows the **flag** on the flagpole.
The wind blows the **kite** in the spring.
The wind blows the **windmill** round and round.
The wind makes the **wind chimes** sing.

The wind blows the **seeds** of the maple tree.
The wind blows the **dust** in a swirl.
The wind blows the **dandelion's** fluffy puff.
The wind makes the **pinwheel** twirl.

—Lucia Kemp Henry

A Counting Rhyme

Reciting a poem, counting 🖥️

In the mood for more poetry? This fun counting rhyme combines math and verse for a hands-on chart activity. Duplicate the appropriate number of the windmill, flag, pinwheel, dandelion, and kite picture cards on page 41 on tagboard. Color the pictures; then laminate them for durability, if desired. Print the counting rhyme on a sheet of poster board. At the end of each line, attach the hook side of a corresponding number of self-adhesive Velcro® dots. Attach the loop side of the Velcro dots to the backs of the picture cards.

Attach all the picture cards at the appropriate places on the poster board. Read through the rhyme once; then go back and count together the pictures at the end of each line. After youngsters are familiar with the poem, leave the chart and picture cards (stored in a resealable plastic bag) available at a center. Students can recite the poem and attach the appropriate picture cards at the end of each line.

One big windmill spinning in the sky,
Two bright flags waving way up high,
Three spinning pinwheels twirling all around,
Four fluffy dandelions blowing near the ground,
Five dancing kites near a tree so tall.
The rushing, whistling wind can blow them all.

—Lucia Kemp Henry

One big windmill
spinning in the sky,

Two bright flags
waving way up
high,

Three spinning pinwheels
twirling all around,

A Windblown Bulletin Board
Demonstrating the effects of moving air

Ask youngsters to help you create this blustery bulletin board with some paint and a little lung power! Cut a length of blue bulletin board paper to fit your bulletin board. When you are ready to begin, give each child a drinking straw. Pour a small puddle of thinned white tempera paint about one foot from the right edge of the paper. Have two students blow through their straws to move the paint toward the paper's right edge. Continue this process—scattering small puddles of paint over the paper—always pouring paint to the *left* and having pairs of youngsters blow the paint to the *right*. Let the paint dry; then staple the paper to your bulletin board. Add a sentence-strip title that reads "Blowin' in the Wind." Then have youngsters help you collect some items that can be wind-blown to display on the board, such as a thin scarf, leaves, a newspaper, and a ball cap.

If desired, snap some photos of your class outside at play on a windy day. Add the photos to the display for a finishing touch.

High-Flying Fun
Following directions, identifying wind direction

No study of wind would be complete without some kite-flying! If you're not proficient at flying a kite yourself, ask another adult to visit your class and demonstrate the technique. Afterward, return to your classroom and engage youngsters in making some simple, tube-shaped kites.

Give each student a sheet of construction paper to decorate as she desires. Provide crayons, markers, stickers, and rubber stamps. Supply crepe paper streamers for children to cut and glue to one long edge of the undecorated side of their papers. Help each child roll her decorated paper into a tube shape and staple it in place. Punch four evenly spaced holes in the end of the tube opposite the streamers. Thread two eight-inch lengths of yarn through the holes so they crisscross and then tie them in place. Finally, tie one end of an 18-inch length of yarn around the center of the crisscross. Head back outside so each student can try her hand at flying her own kite.

Twirling and Whirling

Strengthening the home-school connection

Get parents involved in your study of the wind! For each child, duplicate the parent letter and pinwheel pattern on page 40. Prepare a kraft envelope with take-home materials for each child. Into each child's envelope, place a copy of the letter and pattern, a piece of thick foil gift wrap, an unsharpened pencil, and a pushpin (wrapped securely in a piece of paper to avoid sticking the child). Make sure your youngsters know that the pinwheels are to be assembled with the help of an adult family member.

Encourage little ones to bring their pinwheels back to school the next day so they can check out the power of the wind! If it's not a particularly windy day, use some lung power as a substitute.

People Pinwheels

Recognizing wind blows from a specific direction at any given moment

After making and testing paper pinwheels, invite youngsters to participate in a people pinwheel! Divide your class into groups of five students each. Designate one child in each group to play the part of the Wind and equip him with a cardboard tube. Have the other four students in the group stand in a circle, each with his right hand extended into the center of the circle. Move children close enough so that their extended hands touch—forming the pivot point of the people pinwheel.

Ask the Wind to blow through the tube toward the people pinwheel. Have the children walk around the circle. Invite the Wind to blow softly, then harder, as the children in the people pinwheel try to match his pace. Remind students that without wind the pinwheel can't move, so the children in the pinwheel must pay attention to when the Wind stops blowing. Choose another child to play the part of the Wind and repeat the activity. Continue until each child in each group has had a turn to be the Wind.

Pinwheel Snacks

Following directions

Your youngsters will be all awhirl when they put together these tasty pinwheel-shaped snacks. Have each student spread jam onto a slice of bread. Demonstrate how to cut the bread slice into four triangles as shown. Then invite each child to cut her bread and arrange the four triangles to resemble a pinwheel shape. Have her finish her pinwheel with a round banana slice in its center. Encourage youngsters to enjoy their windy-day snack while listening to a story from "A Blustery Booklist" on page 39.

Breezy Booklets

Showing an understanding of text

Invite your students to create individual booklets using the reproducibles on pages 41–43. Duplicate the picture cards on page 41 and the booklet pages on pages 42 and 43 for each child. Have each child cut apart his booklet pages; then assist him in stacking the pages in order and stapling them along the left edge. Read through the text of the booklet once to familiarize students with it. Then reread each page, stopping at the end of each page to have each child locate, color, and cut out the appropriate picture card from his copy of page 41. Invite him to glue the picture in the open space on the page. After reading the text on the last page, encourage each youngster to color the face to resemble himself—windblown hair and all!

Provide each child with two 7 1/2" x 3 1/2" construction paper rectangles to serve as the front and back covers for his booklet. Print (or have the child copy) the title "The Wind Blows" on his front cover; then staple the covers in place. Invite the children to share their completed booklets with one another before taking them home to read with their families.

The wind blows the flag that floats on the breeze.

The wind blows the leaves that grow on the trees.

The wind blows the hair that grows on me!

The wind blows the chimes that we hear and see.

A Blustery Booklist

Elmer Takes Off
Written by David McKee

Gilberto and the Wind
Written by Marie Hall Ets

The Windy Day
Written by G. Brian Karas

Who Took the Farmer's Hat?
Written by Joan L. Nodset

Dear Family,

At school, we are learning about the wind. Please use the pattern below, the materials in this envelope, and glue and scissors to help your child construct a pinwheel.

1. Glue this paper to the dull side of the sheet of gift wrap.
2. Cut on the bold and dotted lines.
3. Bend the marked corners to the center X.
4. Carefully secure the corners with the pushpin.
5. Push the pushpin partially into the side of the pencil's eraser.

Ask your child to bring the pinwheel back to school tomorrow. We'll test it outside!

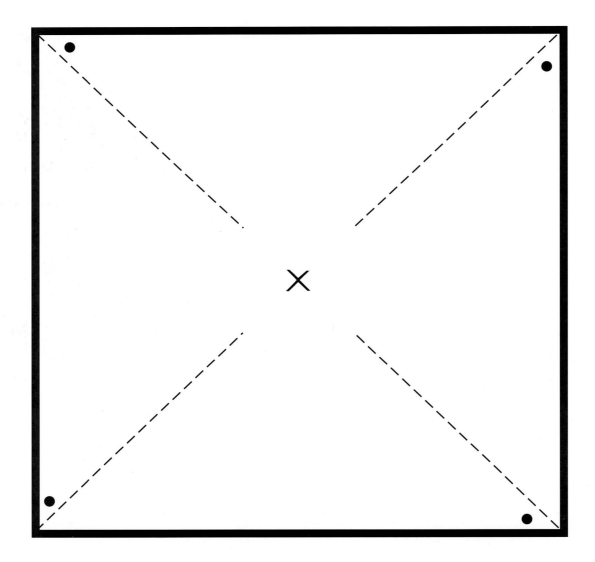

Note to the teacher: Use with "Twirling and Whirling" on page 38.

Picture Cards

Use with "Windy Poetry" and "A Counting Rhyme" on page 36.
and "Breezy Booklets" on page 39.

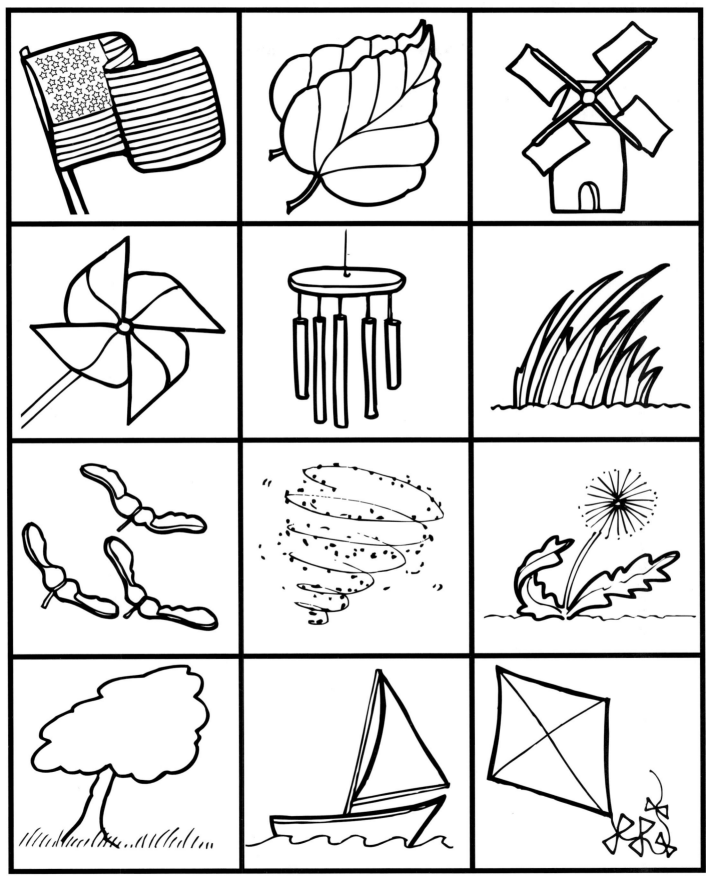

Booklet Pages
Use with "Breezy Booklets" on page 39.

The wind blows
the flag that floats
on the breeze.

1

The wind blows
the leaves
that grow
on the trees.

2

The wind blows
the windmill
that spins
and whirls.

3

The wind blows
the pinwheel
that whirls
and twirls.

4

The wind blows
the chimes
that we
hear and see.

5

The wind blows
the hair
that grows
on me!

6

WILD and

No "lion"! "Ewe" and your little ones will enjoy springing into March with these thematic lion and lamb activities!

So It's Been Said
Collecting, organizing, and interpreting data

Introduce your youngsters to the wacky weather of March by explaining the old saying, "March comes in like a lion and goes out like a lamb." Discuss with your students characteristics of lions (wild and loud) and lambs (quiet and gentle). Then explain that March's weather is wild and ferocious like a lion one day and then gentle and quiet like a lamb the next. Track the changes in March's weather with a duplicated supply of calendar tags using the patterns on page 48. (Or use lion and lamb rubber stamps or stickers for this activity.) Each day during March, discuss the weather and have students decide if it's a "lion day" (cold and windy) or a "lamb day" (warm and sunny). Have a student volunteer use a removable glue stick to attach the appropriate tag to the date on the classroom calendar.

At the end of the month, have children remove the calendar tags and sort them into two groups—lions and lambs. Then create a graph similar to the one shown. Ask students to count the calendar tags in each row. Were there more lion or lamb days in March?

> **March**
> Did we have more lion days or more lamb days?
> Lions
> Lambs
> We had __16__ lion days.
> We had __15__ lamb days
> We had more __lion__ days

Lions and Lambs Math
Extending a pattern, showing understanding of a numeral

Get your students roaring about math with some activities that provide additional uses for the lion and lamb patterns at the top of page 48.

A Pride of Patterns

Supply each child with a 2 1/2" x 9" strip of paper programmed with a pattern (as shown) and a copy of the lion and lamb reproducibles. Have each student continue the pattern by gluing the reproducibles to his strip. Ask more advanced children to create their own lion and lamb patterns.

A Flock of Numbers

Invite your students to match sets and numerals with this nifty number book. Use seven sheets of construction paper to create a book with a cover and six pages. On the front cover, write "Our Lion and Lamb Counting Book." Starting with page one, write "0 Lambs," followed by "1 Lion" on the back of that page. Continue to alternate lions and lambs as the numbers increase to ten.

Then duplicate and cut apart ten copies of the lion and lamb patterns on page 48. On each page, have students identify the numeral and the animal name; then have student volunteers glue the correct number of lions or lambs to the page.

WOOLLY

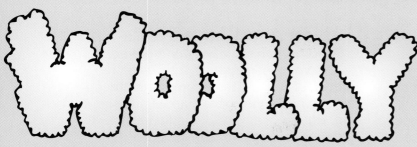

ideas contributed by Mary Sue Chatfield, Ada Hanley Goren, and Sharon Murphy

Lion and Lamb Lore 🖥
Establishing background knowledge

Lion Facts
- Lions are members of the cat family.
- They are large and very strong.
- Only male lions have the thick hair called *manes* on their heads and necks.
- Lions live on grassy plains in groups called *prides*.
- A male is called a *lion,* a female is called a *lioness,* and a baby is called a *cub.*
- Cubs drink a lioness's milk until they are 1 1/2 months old.
- Adults eat zebra, antelope, buffalo, deer, and gazelles.

Lamb Facts
- Lambs are members of the sheep family.
- A male sheep is called a *ram,* a female is called a *ewe,* and a baby is called a *lamb.*
- Sheep live in groups called *flocks* and are usually found in pastures, on farms, and sometimes on dry plains (because they can live without water for long periods of time).
- People raise sheep mainly for food and for their woolly coats.
- Lambs drink their mother's milk.
- Sheep eat grass, grains, hay, wood, and shrubs.

After sharing these facts, divide your little ones into groups of five and invite them to adapt the familiar rhyme "This Little Piggy Went to Market" to fit a lion or a lamb. First, explain to your students that in the original rhyme the first two lines tell where a pig might go, lines three and four tell what a pig might eat, and line five tells the sound a pig makes. Provide help to each group as children work to create either a lion or a lamb rhyme similar to the ones shown. Write each line from each group's rhyme on a lion or lamb cutout or a sheet from a shaped notepad (one line per page). Have each student illustrate one line of her group's poem. Then add covers and staple each group's illustrations together to form booklets.

This little lamb went to the pasture.
This little lamb stayed in the barn.
This little lamb had milk to drink.
This little lamb had grass.
This little lamb cried, "Baa, baa, baa,"
    all the way home.

This little lion went out on the plain.
This little lion stayed with its mother.
This little lion had wildebeest.
This little lion had gazelle.
This little lion cried, "Meow, meow, meow,"
    all the way home.

Lovable Lambs 🖥
Responding to literature

Invite students to read, draw, and write about lambs with this idea. To begin, share with your little ones *Mary Had a Little Lamb* by Sarah J. Hale. This book gives the familiar nursery rhyme a contemporary interpretation with its beautiful photographs. After a first read-through, encourage your youngsters to read (or sing) the first part of it by themselves. Repeated readings will help them become familiar with the additional verses. Next, provide each student with a simple cutout of a lamb. Have students use glue, cotton balls, and construction paper to cover and decorate their lambs as shown.

Near the bottom of an 8 1/2" x 11" piece of white paper, write "_____ had a little lamb"; then make a class supply. Photograph each student holding his lamb. When the photographs have been developed, glue each picture to one of the duplicated sheets. Have each child write his name on the blank. Then have him dictate a second line telling something about his lamb. (Ask more advanced students to dictate some facts they have learned about lambs.) Compile the pages into a class book titled "We All Have Little Lambs."

Lion and Lamb Lyrics 🖥
Building vocabulary, reciting a song

Get your youngsters in tune with the names of lion and lamb family members with some flannelboard cutouts and singing. Duplicate and color the flannelboard patterns on page 48. Laminate the designs before cutting out each one. Attach the hook side of a piece of Velcro® to the back of each design. Now you're ready to get your flannelboard out and start singing these rhymes to the tune of "Row, Row, Row Your Boat."

Sheep, sheep, sheep I see.
Daddy's called a *ram*.
See the mother called a *ewe*,
With her baby *lamb*.

Lions, lions, lions I see,
Together in a *pride*.
Mother's called a *lioness*;
Cubs are by her side.

Masks Worth Roaring About
Developing fine-motor skills

You'll get a roaring response as you nurture students' creative sides with these lion masks. Supply each child with a paper plate (with the inside circle cut out) and ten three-inch squares, each of yellow and brown tissue paper. Instruct each student to place his pointer finger in the middle of a tissue square and wrap the tissue paper around his finger. Next, have him dip his folded tissue in glue and place it on the paper plate. Have him alternate the colors of tissue paper as he continues the pattern around the paper-plate circle. Help each youngster draw and cut out two ears from brown construction paper; then staple them to the top of his paper plate. Use glue or a staple to attach a craft stick. Paint your youngsters' noses with black face paint and have them put on their masks. Then lead your pride of lions on a parade throughout the school!

Wild or Tame?

Understanding basic needs of animals, making comparisons

Reinforce students' classification skills with the lion and lamb theme and two Hula-Hoop® rings. To begin, discuss the words *domesticated* and *wild*. Lambs are domesticated animals. They are cared for by farmers who are responsible for providing food, water, and shelter for them. Lions have to find their own food, water, and shelter; therefore they are considered wild animals. Have your students look through magazines to gather pictures of many different animals. Then place two Hula-Hoop rings on the floor in an overlapping position and label the hoops as shown. As each child shares an animal picture, invite the class to help her decide into which category the picture should be placed. Help your students determine which animals might fall into the overlapping category (such as birds, rabbits, mice, and snakes). Continue this activity until each child has had a chance to share and place a picture.

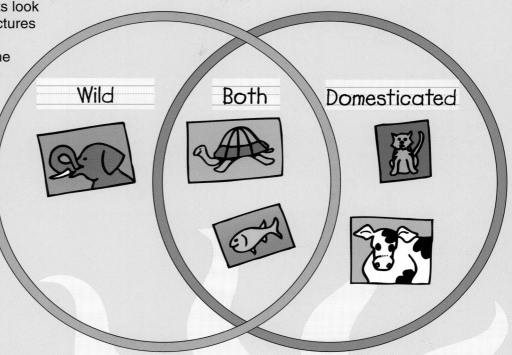

Hungry As a Lion!

Following directions

Celebrate the end of your wild and woolly unit by making lion and lamb cookies. Roll out refrigerated cookie dough, cut into 3 1/2-inch circles, and bake as directed on the package. Then invite your youngsters to add the following ingredients to make these springtime cookies:

Lion Cookies

Ingredients for One:
1 baked sugar cookie
1 vanilla wafer, cut in half
2 tbsp. peanut butter

10 candy corns
3 chocolate chips
chocolate gel icing

Spread the peanut butter over the top of the sugar cookie. Place the vanilla wafer halves at the top of the cookie for the ears. Add candy corn around the edges with the tips pointing inward. Add two chocolate chips for the eyes and one for the nose. Then squeeze the gel icing to form the lion's mouth.

Lamb Cookies

Ingredients for One:
1 baked sugar cookie
1 chocolate wafer, cut in half
1–2 tbsp. marshmallow creme

3 chocolate chips
chocolate gel icing

Spread the marshmallow creme around the edge of the sugar cookie. Place the chocolate wafer halves at the top of the cookie for the ears. Add two chocolate chips for the eyes and one chocolate chip for the nose. Then squeeze the gel icing to form the lamb's mouth.

47

Lion and Lamb Patterns

Use with "So It's Been Said" and "Lions and Lambs Math" on page 44.

Flannelboard Patterns

Use with "Lion and Lamb Lyrics" on page 46.

Nature's Music

Patter-patter. Boom! Roar. Crack! These are only a few of the sounds that contribute to the mystical, magical arrangement of noises created in the great outdoors—nature's music. Invite youngsters to listen to, explore, and re-create some of nature's musical sounds—just for the wonder and fun of it!

by Mackie Rhodes

A Symphony of Animal Sounds
Acknowledging sounds in nature, communicating animal sounds

Some of nature's most beautiful music is made by the creatures of the wild. Recite the following rhyme to youngsters; then repeat each sentence, pausing to allow children the opportunity to provide the sound mentioned for each animal. Conclude the rhyme by inviting students to name additional animals and produce their sounds.

Crickets chirp. Birds tweet.
Chipmunks chatter. Sheep bleat.

Frogs croak. Horses neigh.
Snakes hiss. Donkeys bray.

Elephants trumpet. Mice squeak.
Owls hoot. Peacocks shriek.

Bees buzz. Wolves howl.
Pigs squeal. Bears growl.

Turkeys yelp. Doves coo.
Fish splash. Cows moo.

Cats meow. Ducks quack.
Dogs bark. Camels smack.

Parrots squawk. Lions roar.
Can you think of any more?
—Mackie Rhodes

Echoes Abound
Recognizing that sound travels

Youngsters will enjoy learning about *echoes*—nature's way of repeating its own sounds. To introduce the idea of an echo, read aloud the book *Little Beaver and the Echo* by Amy MacDonald. Then explain that an echo is a sound that bounces back to the person or thing making the sound. Ask children if they have ever heard echoes of their own voices while talking in an empty room.

After a brief discussion about echoes, tell students that many times echoes in nature can be heard where mountains and valleys are found. Then invite youngsters to engage in some echoing activity. Divide the class into two groups of students. Have the groups sit on opposite sides of the room from each other. Assign one group to be the sound source and the other to be the sound's echo. Play the song "Little Sir Echo" from the album *We All Live Together: Volume I* by Greg and Steve (Youngheart Records). During the echoing segments of the songs, point to the appropriately assigned groups to cue them on cupping their hands around their mouths and singing their parts.

If you are unable to obtain this song, invite the sound source group to sing one line at a time of a familiar song—such as "Twinkle, Twinkle, Little Star." Then have the echo group repeat each line of the song to give an echo effect.

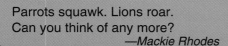

Rhythm of the Rain
Demonstrating a variety of sounds

Saturate youngsters with the many different sounds and rhythms of rain with this rain-making activity. To introduce some rain sounds, read aloud *Listen to the Rain* by Bill Martin Jr. and John Archambault. Then invite youngsters to make their own rain rhythms—by snapping fingers, clapping knees, tapping toes, clicking tongues, clapping hands, or using any other body parts to simulate the sound of falling rain. To begin, produce a simple rainfall rhythm for youngsters to repeat. Then ask students to repeat, in follow-the-leader fashion, a rhythm produced by a volunteer—the rainmaker. Give each child the opportunity to be the rainmaker. Conclude the activity by inviting each child to make rain sounds using the method of his choice. This will be one rainstorm you'll not want to stop!

Wind Song 🖥
Communicating how sounds vary in pitch and volume

Making these wind tubes with which to produce the voices of the wind will be a breeze for little ones! To make a tube, have a child glue short tissue paper or cellophane strips to one end of a short cardboard tube. After the glue dries, ask the child to blow into the other end of the tube to produce wind and to make the paper strips move. Then explain that the wind makes many different sounds—it has many voices. Teach youngsters this song about the voices of the wind. Each time a verse is sung, encourage students to make the suggested wind sound. Sing the song once; then repeat the song, each time replacing the underlined words with one of the following and its corresponding sound: *howl, moan,* or *roar.*

The Wind's Voices
(sung to the tune of "Frère Jacques")

"I can [whisper]. I can [whisper],"
Says the wind, says the wind.
"Shhhhh…
Shhhhh,"
Says the wind, says the wind.

A Fallen Tree
Dramatizing with sound and creative movement

Invite students to imitate the sound of a tree as it cracks and falls to the ground with this song involving movement. Obtain a recording of the song "A Tree Fell Down" from the album *Easy Does It* by Hap Palmer. Then convert a simple broom into a tree by using twist ties to attach large stems of artificial leaves (available at craft stores) to the straw end of the broom. Divide the students in your class into two groups. Give each student in one group a pair of rhythm sticks. Have the other group form a line near a volunteer holding the tree. Then play the song. Each time the song refers to the *crack* of the tree, have the group with the rhythm sticks strike their sticks together to represent that sound. Also instruct the child holding the tree to let it fall to the ground. Then have him hold the tree in a horizontal position to allow the other group of children to maneuver past it in the way suggested in the song. As student interest dictates, repeat the song and activity, switching the roles of the groups and inviting a different volunteer to hold the tree each time. If you are unable to obtain a recording of the song, cue students to make the tree crack and fall to the ground; then instruct them on ways to maneuver over and under the fallen tree, such as jumping over or crawling under it.

Thunderstorm
Connecting volume and energy

A thunderstorm will parade through your classroom when youngsters explore different ways to imitate the sounds of thunder. Provide a number of different types of thunder-producing instruments, such as drums, wood blocks, and tambourines. Invite students to take turns experimenting with these instruments to make sounds similar to thunder—consecutive beatings on the drum to create rolling thunder, striking the wood block once to simulate a thunderclap, and striking the tambourine to create a crackle of thunder. Then challenge the children to create thunder at different volumes. Afterward, have the students line up with their instruments in parade formation to participate in a thunderous parade around the classroom.

Literature Links to Nature's Lyrics

The sounds of nature have so fascinated people that books abound on this topic. Share some of these books and related activities with your students; then invite them to visit their local libraries to discover the windfall of books that awaits them there.

Mice Squeak, We Speak
by Tomie dePaola
Responding to literature, representing an oral message in writing

This book entices youngsters not only to *listen* to the sounds made by a variety of animals but also to produce those sounds themselves. Read the story aloud to youngsters once, and then again, encouraging them to participate in the reading and sound effects corresponding to the book. Afterward, invite the children to make a class big book about animal sounds. Give each child two large sheets of construction paper. Ask him to illustrate an animal on one of his papers. At the bottom of his page, write his dictation about the sound his animal makes, using the sentences, "This is my [name of animal]. It can [name of animal sound]." Then help the child write that sound on his other sheet of paper. Encourage him to use lettering that represents the sound—for instance, large bold letters might represent a bear's *growl,* while small letters might be used for a bird's *tweet.* Sequence each child's word page behind his illustrated page; then stack all the pages together. Bind the pages between two construction paper covers. Write the title "Animals Speak" on the front cover; then place the book in the reading center for students to enjoy.

Barnyard Banter
by Denise Fleming
Participating in storytelling

Delight youngsters with this colorful book filled with barnyard sounds and a hidden surprise on every page. Before reading the book aloud, invite each child to make a goose finger puppet. Duplicate the puppet pattern on page 53 on tagboard for each child. Have the child cut out his pattern; then help him as necessary to cut out the holes for the beak. Next, have him color his cutout and draw eyes (or glue on wiggle eyes). Ask the children to place their puppets on their fingers and then hold them behind their backs as the book is read. As you read the words aloud, invite youngsters to chime in whenever an animal sound is mentioned. When the last page is read, encourage each child to *honk* while he brings his puppet out from behind his back. There's a goose—honking up a storm of beautiful music!

More Books to Hear About

Polar Bear, Polar Bear, What Do You Hear?
Written by Bill Martin, Jr.

The Very Quiet Cricket
Written by Eric Carle

What Does the Rabbit Say?
Written by Jacque Hall

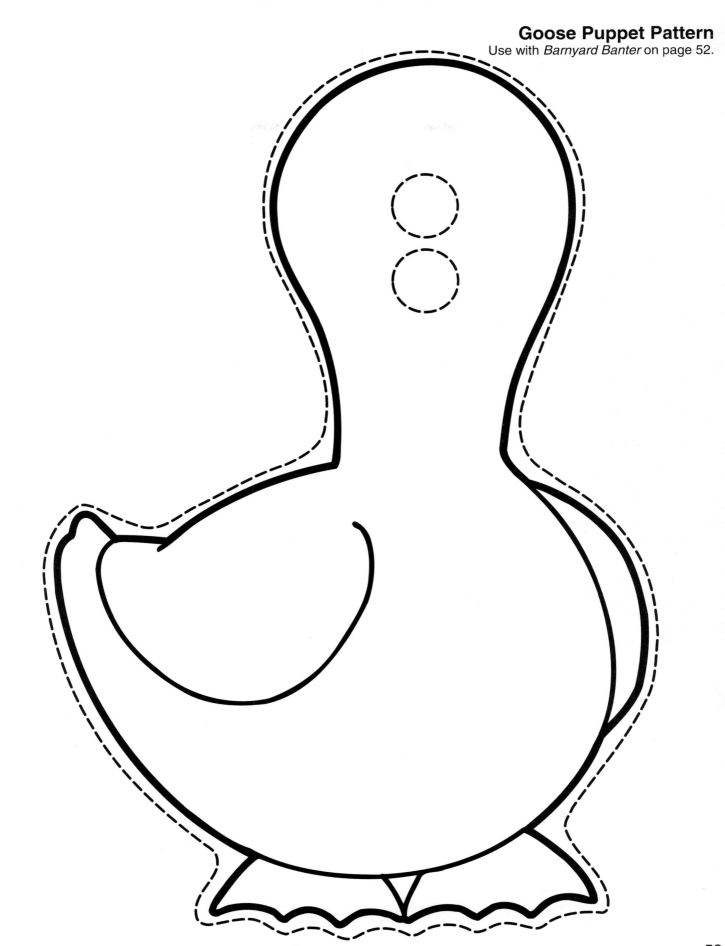

Designed to Delight: Clothing Activities for Children

Try these clothing ideas to promote cross-curricular learning along with a lot of practice in independent dressing skills. Pretty soon, your youngsters will be dressed for success!

ideas contributed by Christina Boyd and Mackie Rhodes

Wonderful World of Wearables

Understanding clothing and its purpose

Welcome youngsters into the wonderful world of wearables by setting up a dress-up center in your classroom. Place dressing-related furnishings in the center—such as a set of drawers, a portable closet, a clothes tree, and a full-length mirror. Gather an assortment of clothes, a few sizes larger than your students' own clothing, to represent articles worn in all kinds of weather and places. Put these—as well as a variety of costumes, uniforms, and accessories, such as mittens, caps, and shoes—in the center. Invite each youngster to engage in some dress-up fun while visiting the center; then take his photo. Write the child's dictation about his dress-up outfit on a sentence strip. Display the child's photo with his dictation on a clothes-covered bulletin board titled "Wonderful Wearables." Encourage youngsters to visit the dress-up center often to practice dressing-related skills—such as matching clothes, manipulating fasteners, and independent dressing.

Fabulous Fad of the Day

Describing similarities and differences

Students will enjoy participating in the fad of the day when they dress for these special days. Choose several dates during your planned clothing unit; then designate a Fad of the Day—stripes, polka dots, silly hats, etc.—for each date. Prior to your first Fad Day, duplicate one copy of the parent letter on page 60. Program the copy with the desired information; then duplicate that copy to be sent home with each child. For each Fad Day, ask youngsters to wear the suggested clothes or design for that day. Have the children discuss the similarities and differences between their clothes. Then take a group picture of the class, as well as a few other pictures throughout the day. Mount the pictures on a photo-album page labeled with that day's special clothes or design, such as "Polka-Dot Day." Title the album "Our Fad Days" and place it in the reading center for students to enjoy.

Dear Parent,

Do you recall some of the clothing fads of your day? If so, you'll enjoy helping your own child dress for our class Fad Days during our study of clothing. Please refer to the list below and have your child wear something that corresponds to the suggestion for each Fad Day. We will discuss the similarities and differences in our clothes, and take pictures to include in a class book. We look forward to our Fad Days—days filled with fabulous fads and fun!

Dates:
March 10
March 11
March 12
March 13
March 14

Clothing:
something plaid
hats
polka dots
silly socks
stripes

As always, your cooperation and support are appreciated!

Hokey-Pokey Clothes

Identifying articles of clothing, dramatizing a song

Delight youngsters with a stylish new dance—the Hokey-Pokey Clothes Dance! For each child, duplicate the parent request letter on page 60. Using the list in the letter, prepare a few additional sets of clothes for students who forget to bring theirs or do not have extra clothes sets available. After the students have brought the requested clothes, have them form a circle. Ask each child to place his clothes set behind him. While singing each verse, have him pick up and "dance" the clothing item mentioned in that verse. On the last beat of the verse, name one of the following to indicate the next item to be used: *pants, shorts, socks, shoes, hat/cap, shirt.* Then repeat the song, replacing the repeated underlined word with the last item named.

(sung to the tune of "The Hokey-Pokey")

You put your [shirt] in.
You take your [shirt] out.
You put your [shirt] in
And you shake it all about.
You do the Hokey-Pokey,
And you move your clothes around.
That's what it's all about! [Pants]!

A Model Example

Modeling spatial arrangements

Youngsters will learn a lot about positioning and spatial arrangements from these clothes models. Divide your class into groups of four or five students. Have the students in one group sit on the floor facing you. Ask each child to place her set of clothes (from "Hokey-Pokey Clothes") behind her. From a similar set of clothes, arrange one of the items, such as a pair of pants, in a particular way (for example, with one leg folded upward and the other laid out straight). Explain that this is the clothes model. Then ask each student to find a similar article of clothing in her set and to arrange that item so that it resembles the model. After repeating the activity several times with different clothing items, invite each child in turn to position a clothing model for the other group members to imitate.

Hanging Around

Developing fine-motor skills, sorting

While they still have their clothes sets out (from "Hokey-Pokey Clothes"), why not have youngsters hang them up for a little sorting fun? To prepare, set up a clothesline in your classroom. Provide a supply of rubber-coated clothes hangers and some spring-type clothespins. Invite each youngster in a small group to fit or clip each of his clothing items onto a separate hanger (except his shoes, of course!). Then have him place the hangers on the clothesline. When all the clothes are hanging, encourage each child, in turn, to sort them by color or by the kind of item.

Pocket Pass

Using sense of touch to analyze and identify objects

Of all the different parts of a clothing item, the pocket is probably the most interesting—and certainly the most fun to fill! Invite youngsters to play a Hot Potato–style pocket game that will encourage them to stay alert and engage in problem solving. To prepare, cut out a button or snap pocket through all thicknesses of an old shirt or jacket. Gather a supply of small common objects, such as a one-inch cube, a teddy-bear counter, a coin, and a plastic spoon. Place one item in the pocket; then fasten the pocket closed so that the item stays inside it. During group time, ask students to brainstorm a list of things that can be put in a pocket. After the discussion, encourage each student, in turn, to examine her clothes for pockets and then count them.

Then invite the class to play the Pocket Pass game. Ask the students to form a circle. On the signal "Go" have the students pass the pocket around the circle as in a game of Hot Potato. On the signal "Stop" ask the child holding the pocket to feel the object through the fabric and then try to guess what is hidden inside. If necessary, provide clues until the child correctly identifies the item. Then, out of the view of your students, remove that item and replace it with another. Repeat the game, playing as long as student interest dictates.

Pick a Pocket

Increasing visual memory

One of the greatest challenges in having lots of pockets in your clothing is to remember which items are in which pockets. Use this pocket memory game to help youngsters practice using their visual memory skills. To prepare the gameboard, duplicate the shirt-and-pocket pattern on page 61. Use an opaque projector to enlarge the shirt-pattern outline on a sheet of poster board. Copy the pocket pattern on a sheet of tagboard; then cut out the pattern. Use this cutout as a template to trace 12 pocket outlines on felt sheets. Cut out the felt pockets; then hot-glue each pocket along its sides and bottom edges only onto the poster board shirt. Collect six pairs of small objects in which each item in a pair is identical. Out of your students' view, place one of these objects into each of the pockets on the gameboard.

To play, ask a student in a small group to remove the items from two different pockets on the board. If the items match, the student may keep them. If they are not identical, have the student return each item to its pocket; then continue play in the same manner with the next child in the group. Invite each youngster in turn to check two pockets until all the item pairs have been found. Return each item to a pocket on the gameboard; then invite another group of students to play.

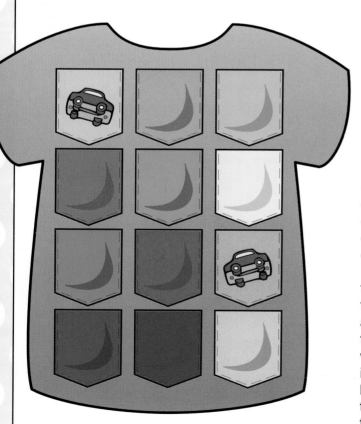

Button Away!

Developing fine-motor skills, reciting and dramatizing a rhyme

Youngsters will be eager to fasten buttons to create a BIG shirt with rhyming fun up its sleeves! Collect four front-buttoning shirts (youth or small adult sizes are best) that have the same number of similar-size buttons on the same side of each shirt—either on the left placket or the right. Spread out the shirts side by side with the outside of the fabric facing up. Line up the button placket of each shirt with the buttonhole placket of the neighboring shirt. Invite each child in a group of three to fasten the buttons of one shirt into the buttonholes of the shirt beside it. After the students complete their buttoning, have each child insert his arms into the sleeves of one of the shirts that make up the resulting big shirt. Then either slip your arms into the two remaining sleeves or select an additional child to do so. Encourage the youngsters wearing the big shirt to perform the actions as they recite this rhyme. Afterward, have them remove the big shirt and unfasten the buttons. Then ask them to pass the four shirts on to the next trio of students for them to assemble into a big shirt.

Sleeves go up. Sleeves go down.
Sleeves go round and round and round.

Sleeves go up. Sleeves go down.
Now everybody sit down!

Measurement With a Zip

Using manipulatives to measure length, ordering numbers

Z-z-zip into measurement skills with this unique activity. Gather an assortment of clothes with zipper closures, such as pants, jackets, and vests. Provide a supply of one-inch cubes and sticky notes. Have students pair off; then invite each pair to select a clothing item from the collection. Instruct the students to measure the length of that item's zipper with the cubes. Then have one of the partners write the number of cubes used on a sticky note and attach it to the item. As a class, sequence the clothes by zipper lengths using the numeral-labeled sticky notes as a guide. What "zipper-dee-doo-dah" fun!

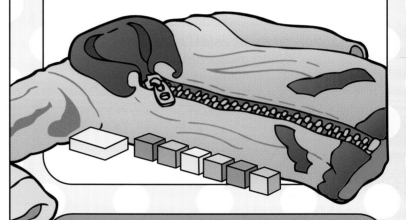

"Fasten-ating" Surprises

Developing fine-motor skills

Entice little ones to work on their fastening skills with these fun-filled surprise packages. Gather an assortment of clothes, making sure that many different types of fasteners are represented in the collection—zippers, laces, snaps, buttons, Velcro® closures, and hooks. Also gather a variety of packages and clothes-related containers—such as shirt boxes, suitcases, laundry bags, and decorative shopping bags. Place one clothing article in each package. During center time, or when there are a few extra minutes to fill, invite each student to select one of the packages. Have him remove the item from the package and then practice fastening and unfastening the closure. After he finishes, ask him to return the item to the package.

What Shall I Wear?

Making appropriate clothing choices

Encourage little ones to become independent in their clothes selections for various occasions and weather conditions with this activity. To prepare, duplicate the picture cards on page 62 onto tagboard. If desired, color the cards; then laminate them for durability. Provide several suitcases filled with an assortment of clothes, such as those gathered for "Wonderful World of Wearables" on page 54 and "Hokey-Pokey Clothes" on page 55—making sure to include appropriate clothing to correspond to each picture card. Invite each youngster, in turn, to select a picture card, then find and either show or put on clothes that are appropriate for that occasion. Write this child's dictated statement about his clothing choices on a sentence strip. Display each child's sentence strip with an enlarged copy of the corresponding picture card. Title the display "What Shall I Wear?"

Sock Hop

Matching by physical attributes, developing gross-motor skills

Sock some matching skills your students' way with this game that will keep 'em hopping. Collect the same number of sock pairs as students in your class. Find sock pairs that differ in some way—such as size, color, or weave pattern—so that no two pairs are identical. Place one sock from each pair in a laundry basket. Have the students sit in a circle around the basket; then give each child one of the remaining socks. Ask each student to place the sock behind him on the floor. Invite a volunteer to close his eyes and pick a sock from the basket; then, starting from where he is seated, have him hop on one foot around the outside of the circle looking for the mate to his sock. When he finds it, instruct him to pick up the mate and then jump on both feet back to his seat. Give every child an opportunity to play the game in the same manner—hopping on one foot when he has only one sock and then jumping on both feet when he is holding the pair. After all the sock pairs have been found, ask each child to fold his socks together. Then invite each child in turn to hop to the basket to return his sock pair.

Shoe Count

Showing an understanding of a numeral

So many shoes! So many different uses for them! To prepare this step-lively game of counting excitement, gather ten lidded shoeboxes and ten pairs of different kinds of footwear, such as football cleats, tap shoes, rubber boots, and bedroom slippers. Then place each pair of footwear in an appropriately sized box. Attach a card labeled with a different numeral from 1 to 10 on each shoebox lid; then place each lid on its corresponding box.

Read aloud *Whose Shoe?* by Margaret Miller. Afterward, ask students to name any other types of footwear they can think of. Then assign each of ten children a number from 1 to 10. Invite her to take a turn finding the shoebox labeled with her assigned number; then have the child put on the shoes from her box. Challenge her to take the number of steps that corresponds to the box label, and some interesting footwork may be the result! Then have her return the footwear to the box. Give each child an opportunity to participate; then play another round, assigning a different number to each child.

Weaving Workout

Making and stating observations, working cooperatively

Exercise students' thinking skills with a weaving workout that will give them firsthand experience with how fabric is made. To introduce the concept of *weaving,* give each child a square of burlap to examine. Ask him to pull a few of the threads to see what happens. Discuss the children's observations; then explain that the threads are woven under and over one another to create a piece of cloth. To demonstrate a weave pattern, invite six volunteers to stand side by side to represent threads. Tie one end of a roll of crepe paper streamer to the ankle of the child at the end. Then have two other children work together to weave the streamer alternately in front of and then behind the row of children until the pair reaches the last child. Instruct them to wrap the streamer around that child; then turn the roll over to two different students to weave in the opposite direction. Continue having more pairs of students weave the streamer through the row of children until a weave pattern has been created from their ankles to their shoulders. Then challenge the children who are part of the weave to try to move. What happens? Explain that it is difficult for any of them to move independently because the interlocking "threads" hold them in place—just like the threads in a piece of fabric. Finally, invite the youngsters to break out of their weave. If desired, repeat the activity with different students.

Fashionable Fabrics

Describing texture and appearance of clothing

Encourage each youngster to explore fabric textures as he makes a picture for a class book. To prepare, cut a supply of small squares from a variety of fabrics with different textures, such as burlap, tulle, seersucker, and a knit. For each child, duplicate the clothes patterns on page 63 onto construction paper. Have the child draw the head, hands, and feet on the picture. Then invite him to glue fabric squares onto the shirt and pants outlines to create his own designs. Write his dictated statement about the textures and looks of his creation on a strip of paper. Stack the students' pages together and bind them between two construction paper covers. Then glue each child's strip on the back of the page before his own so that the text is on the left and the picture is on the right. Write the title "Fashion Statements" on the front cover; then invite student pairs to read the book together.

Stupendous Styles

Using art media, using descriptive language

If your students have a flair for fashion, now's the time to let it shine! Invite youngsters to create their own fashion designs to show off in a fashion show. Provide youngsters with large paper bags, various lengths of fabric, lots of collage materials, a variety of fasteners, glue, and scissors. Encourage each child to use these materials to design and create an article of clothing. Then write his dictated description of his creation on an index card. A few days prior to the show, make one copy of the invitation on page 62. Program this copy; then duplicate a class quantity. Send one home with each child. On the day of the show, have youngsters don their designs. Encourage each child, in turn, to model his creation while you read his description to the audience. After this fun fashion finale, serve light refreshments to all.

Parent Letter

Use with "Fabulous Fad of the Day" on page 54.

Dear Parent,

Do you recall some of the clothing fads of your day? If so, you'll enjoy helping your own child dress for our class Fad Days during our study of clothing. Please refer to the list below and have your child wear something that corresponds to the suggestion for each Fad Day. We will discuss the similarities and differences in our clothes, and take pictures to include in a class book. We look forward to our Fad Days—days filled with fabulous fads and fun!

Dates: Clothing:

As always, your cooperation and support are appreciated!

©The Education Center, Inc. • *MARCH* • TEC247

Parent Request Letter

Use with "Hokey-Pokey Clothes" on page 55.

Dear Parent,

During our study of clothing, we will be participating in activities that require the use of several different articles of clothing. Please send in the following items for your child. Please label each item with your child's name or initials. After completing our clothing studies, the items will be returned home. Thank you for your assistance in making our clothing unit fun and relevant!

Please send the following clothing items by _____:
                                                                    (date)

short-sleeved shirt
long-sleeved shirt
pair of pants
pair of shorts
pair of socks
pair of shoes
hat or cap

©The Education Center, Inc. • *MARCH* • TEC247

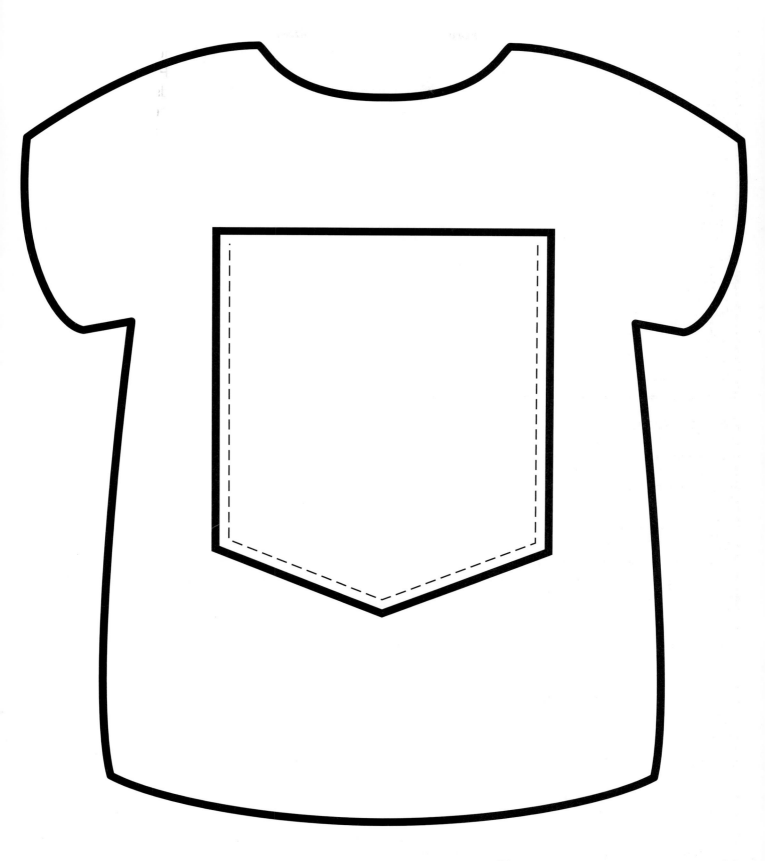

Picture Cards

Use with "What Shall I Wear?" on page 58.

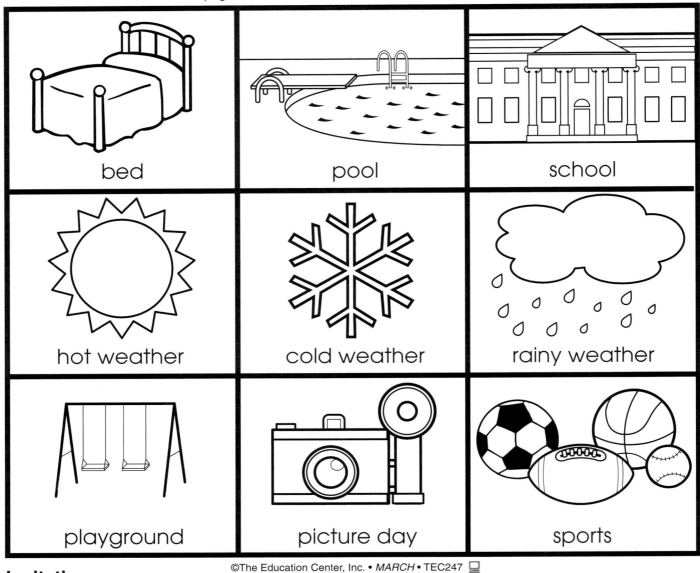

bed

pool

school

hot weather

cold weather

rainy weather

playground

picture day

sports

Invitation

Use with "Stupendous Styles" on page 59.

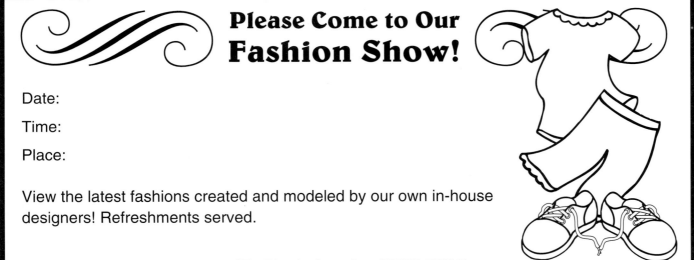

Please Come to Our Fashion Show!

Date:

Time:

Place:

View the latest fashions created and modeled by our own in-house designers! Refreshments served.

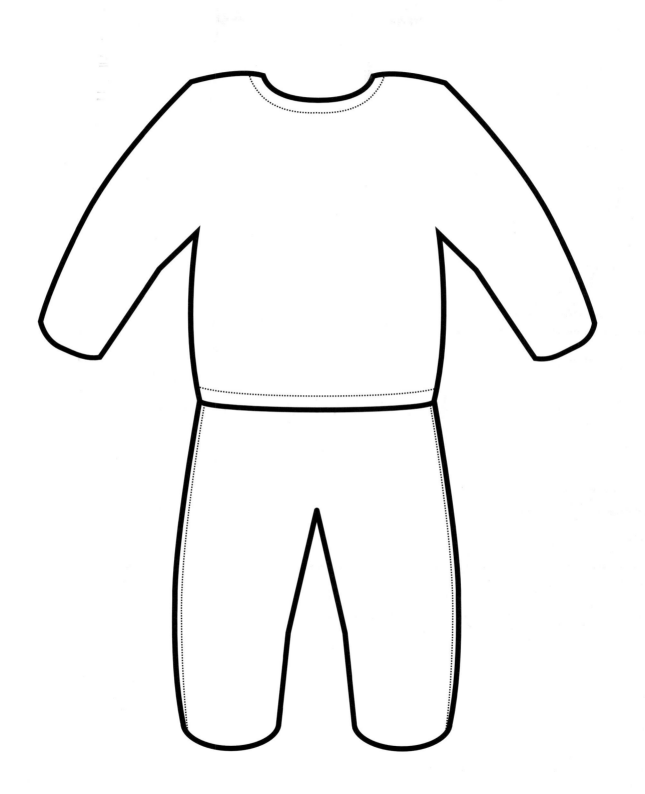

GO HOG-WILD!

From their silly-looking snouts to their cute curly tails, pigs are precious! Here are some "hand-pigged" activities involving science, music, language, cooking, and art to help your little ones learn about the oh-so-fine swine!

ideas contributed by Jan Brennan and Ada Hanley Goren

PIGGY FACTS
Establishing background knowledge

Begin your study of pigs by reading *All Pigs Are Beautiful* by Dick King-Smith. This book describes the author's personal pig fancy and throws in some interesting facts, too. Discuss the information contained in the book; then share some more fascinating facts about pigs with your youngsters:

- Pigs are smart. A pig can be housebroken and taught to walk on a leash or do tricks—just like a dog.
- Piglets weigh about 2 1/2 pounds when they are born. They gain weight very quickly. By the time a pig is six months old, it can weigh over 200 pounds! A fully grown pig weighs between 300 and 500 pounds.
- Some people think pigs are dirty, because they like to roll in the mud. But pigs roll in mud to help them cool off and to protect their skin from sunburn. They actually keep themselves cleaner than most other farm animals.
- Humans use almost every part of the pig. Besides eating its meat, people use other parts of the pig to make medicines, brushes, soap, glue, and leather.

PIG TALK 🖥
Building vocabulary, reciting a poem

Familiarize your students with some piggy vocabulary with this variation of the traditional poem "To Market, to Market."

To market, to market, to buy a fat pig;
Home again, home again, jiggety jig.
To market, to market, to buy a fat hog;
Home again, home again, jiggety jog.

Are a *pig* and a *hog* the same, these two?
Here's what I know; I'll share it with you.
A pig is a youngster, but then when he's grown:
A pig **or** a hog—that's how he's known.

To market, to market, to buy a fat sow;
Home again, home again, jiggety jow.
To market, to market, to buy a fat boar;
Home again, home again, jiggety joar.

Are a *sow* and a *boar* the same, these two?
Here's what I know; I'll share it with you.
They're both as different as different can be:
A sow is a she and a boar is a he.

THE HIGGY-PIGGY
Building vocabulary with song and dance

Introduce your little ones to more pig vocabulary with a movement activity that involves some piggy parts! Before teaching little ones this song, discuss the terms *hoof, hamhock,* and *snout.* Then ask students to stand in a circle and follow your lead as you perform this variation of the traditional Hokey-Pokey.

You put your right hoof in;
You put your right hoof out;
You put your right hoof in and
   you shake it all about.
You do the Higgy-Piggy,
And you turn yourself around.
That's what it's all about!
Oink!

Continue the song-and-dance routine
with the following verses:
   You put your left hoof in…
   You put your right hamhock (hip) in…
   You put your left hamhock in…
   You put your snout in…
   You put your curly tail in…

VALUABLE SNOUTS
Understanding animal behavior, using senses to gather information

Pigs have a keen sense of smell. They use their snouts to sniff out and root for food under the ground. In France and Italy, pigs are especially prized for their ability to locate very expensive and precious truffles that grow as far as 20 feet underground! Invite your students to imitate super-sniffing pigs with this fun activity.

In advance, make a class supply of the snout patterns on page 70 on pink construction paper. Encourage each child to cut out a snout and punch holes where indicated. Then help each youngster thread the ends of a length of elastic through the holes and tie them securely. Invite the children to don their pig snouts and admire their new noses in a mirror. While your costumed piggies are visiting centers or otherwise occupied, prepare several plates of foods that have strong smells, such as peanut butter on crackers, fresh green pepper slices, orange sections, banana slices, chocolate candy pieces, mint candies, and gingerbread cookies. Place a clean napkin or a paper towel over each plate.

Set the covered plates on a tabletop and call a small group of piggies to participate. Invite one child at a time to choose a plate to sniff. Ask him to identify the food under the cover; then uncover the plate to see if his answer was correct. Invite the child to take a sample from the plate to taste. After each child in the group has had a turn, invite another group to test their super snouts!

PIGGY POEMS AND STORIES 💻
Dramatizing select characters

There are many stories and rhymes that your little actors and actresses will enjoy dramatizing. Prepare pig snouts following the directions given in "Valuable Snouts" on page 65. Then ask youngsters to don their snouts and take turns acting out the classic story *The Three Little Pigs.* Provide some simple props, such as raffia (to represent straw), twigs (sticks, of course), and wooden blocks wrapped in red bulletin board paper (to represent bricks).

After each child has had a turn to portray a piggy from the classic fairy tale, arrange to dramatize the traditional nursery rhyme "This Little Piggy Went to Market." And, if your little ones are still in the mood for drama, try singing this variation of the traditional song "The Ants Go Marching One by One." Encourage youngsters to line up single file, and then in pairs, trios, and quartets—singing the verses and marching around the room. Designate a different child to serve as "the little one" in each verse.

THE PIGS GO MARCHING ONE BY ONE
The pigs go marching [one] by [one].
Oink-oink! Oink-oink!
The pigs go marching [one] by [one].
Oink-oink! Oink-oink!

The pigs go marching [one] by [one].
The little one stopped to [eat a bun],
And they all go marching around their pen.
And they want to march again;
Oink, oink, oink!

Continue the song, replacing the underlined number word with two, three, *and* four, *and replacing the underlined phrase with a corresponding phrase from the list below:*

two—chew and chew
three—say, "Look at me!"
four—eat some more

GREAT PIG PICKS AT THE LIBRARY

The Piggy in the Puddle
Written by Charlotte Pomerantz

A Treeful of Pigs
Written by Arnold Lobel

The Three Little Pigs
Retold by James Marshall

Perfect the Pig
Written by Susan Jeschke

Mrs. Potter's Pig
Written by Phyllis Root

Pigs Aplenty, Pigs Galore!
Written by David McPhail

FINE SWINE TALES
Promoting an enjoyment of books

Pigs have been popular characters in children's books for a long time. Suggest that your little ones root out some piggy literature on their next family trip to the library. To remind them and to educate parents about some great pig picks, duplicate the pig bookmarks on page 71 onto pink paper so that each student has one to take home.

MANNERLY SWINE
Understanding good manners

Because of the misconception that many people have about pigs being dirty, our friends the hogs have become the source of several expressions with negative connotations. Your little ones may have heard people say things like "He eats like a pig!" or "This place is a pigsty!" Discuss the meanings of these phrases; then talk with youngsters about manners. Share the book *Perfect Pigs: An Introduction to Manners* by Marc Brown and Stephen Krensky. Good manners in a lot of different situations are illustrated in this book, so you may want to share it in several sessions.

After reading this book, involve your little ones in making their own book of manners. Ask each youngster to recall one statement about good manners. Write his statement on a speech-bubble cutout. Once again, use the snouts made in "Valuable Snouts" on page 65 or "Piggy Poems and Stories" on page 66. Have each youngster put on her snout; then take her photo. Give each child her developed photo and her speech bubble to glue on a sheet of construction paper as shown. Stack all the pages together between construction paper covers. Write "Perfect Pigs: Our Class Book of Manners" on the cover. Place the book in your reading center for children to enjoy.

MARVELOUS MUD
Participating in a sensory experience

Pigs may not be dirty, but they do indeed enjoy a good mud puddle! And your youngsters will enjoy this sensory experience involving imitation mud. In advance, purchase and prepare several packages of instant chocolate pudding. Spoon about 1/4 cup of pudding onto a plastic plate for each child. Then invite youngsters to hoof it over to a tabletop center to make some mud masterpieces! Encourage youngsters to fingerpaint pictures, numerals, letters, words, or shapes in the pudding.

If they are available, provide small, plastic pig counters along with the plates of mud. Ask youngsters to use the pig counters to illustrate math problems, such as "Two pigs were in the mud puddle. Along came three more. How many pigs were in the mud?" Provide a tub of water and some disposable wipes at the end of this activity. Ask each youngster to drop her messy pig counters into the tub of water (to prevent them from escaping down your classroom sink's drain); then have her clean her fingers with a wipe on the way to a more thorough hand-washing.

PIGGY BANKS
Understanding the concept of saving money for future needs

Many young children have had the experience of saving coins in a piggy bank. But did you ever wonder how the tradition of piggy banks started? Thousands of years ago, a type of clay known as *pygg* was used to make dishes, pots, and jars. People saved their money in these jars and started calling them *pygg banks.* When people started asking potters to make pygg banks, the potters misunderstood and created pig-shaped jars. And the piggy bank was born!

Invite your students to make their own piggy banks from toilet tissue tubes. In advance, make a class supply of the patterns on page 72 on pink construction paper. For each child, provide a tube with a slot cut on one side as shown. Invite the children to paint their tubes with pink tempera paint. Set the tubes aside to dry. Then give each child a set of the duplicated patterns. Assist each child in cutting out his patterns and in using a hole puncher to make a hole in the center of the plain circle. Have each child twist one-half of a pink pipe cleaner around his finger to create a curly pig tail. Insert one end of the curly tail into the punched hole; then bend and tape it in place on the back of the circle. Help each student glue the tail, head, and four legs onto his tube to create a piggy bank. Encourage each child to take his bank home to share with his family.

PIGGY-BANK PRACTICE 🖥
Showing an understanding of a numeral

Of course, no piggy bank is complete without some money to go inside! Use the piggy-bank pattern on page 73 to create a center where little ones can use real pennies for counting practice. Make as many copies of the piggy-bank pattern as desired on tagboard. Cut out the patterns and label each of them but one with a different numeral. (Choose numbers that will be appropriate for your students' ability levels.) Laminate these patterns for durability, if desired. Glue the unlabeled cutout on the front of a string-tie envelope, and write the title "Put the Pennies in the Piggy Banks" on this cutout. Place all the numbered cutouts inside the envelope, along with a resealable plastic bag containing a large supply of pennies. To use this center, a child identifies the numeral on each bank and places the corresponding number of pennies "in" that bank.

PIGS IN BLANKETS
Following directions

People love pigs for many reasons—a very important one being that many kinds of meat come from a pig. Pigs are the source of ham, bacon, pork chops, sausage, and some ribs and hot dogs. Try making this twist on the traditional pig in a blanket for a tasty pig treat your little ones will enjoy. (As always, check for food allergies and restrictions before serving food to your students.)

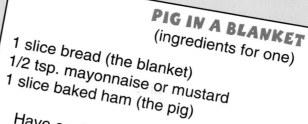

PIG IN A BLANKET
(ingredients for one)

1 slice bread (the blanket)
1/2 tsp. mayonnaise or mustard
1 slice baked ham (the pig)

Have each child wash his hands. Then give him a slice of bread on a paper plate. Have him use a small rolling pin or his hands to press down on the bread and flatten it. Provide the mayonnaise or mustard to spread over his flattened bread. Then have each student place his slice of ham atop his bread. Demonstrate how to roll the bread and ham into a log shape. Ta da—a pig in a blanket!

PIG FOOD
Following directions

OK—we know that people eat pigs, but what do pigs eat? The answer is—just about anything! Pigs on farms usually eat *grain mash* (a combination of oats, corn, and barley mixed with water or milk), all kinds of vegetables, and kitchen scraps. Thrown all together, this is known as *slops*. Undomesticated pigs will eat worms, chestnuts, roots, acorns, and other foods they can find in the woods.

Ask your little ones if they'd like to "eat like pigs" one day; then have them assist you in preparing this fun version of slops!

SLOPS
(makes 24 half-cup servings)

6 c. vanilla yogurt
3 c. cut-up fruit
3 c. crunchy granola
1 c. grated carrots
1 c. nuts

Mix together all the ingredients. Spoon servings into individual paper cups and invite children to "eat like pigs"! (Actually have them use spoons and use their best manners.)

Snout Patterns

Use with "Valuable Snouts" on page 65, "Piggy Poems and Stories" on page 66, and "Mannerly Swine" on page 67.

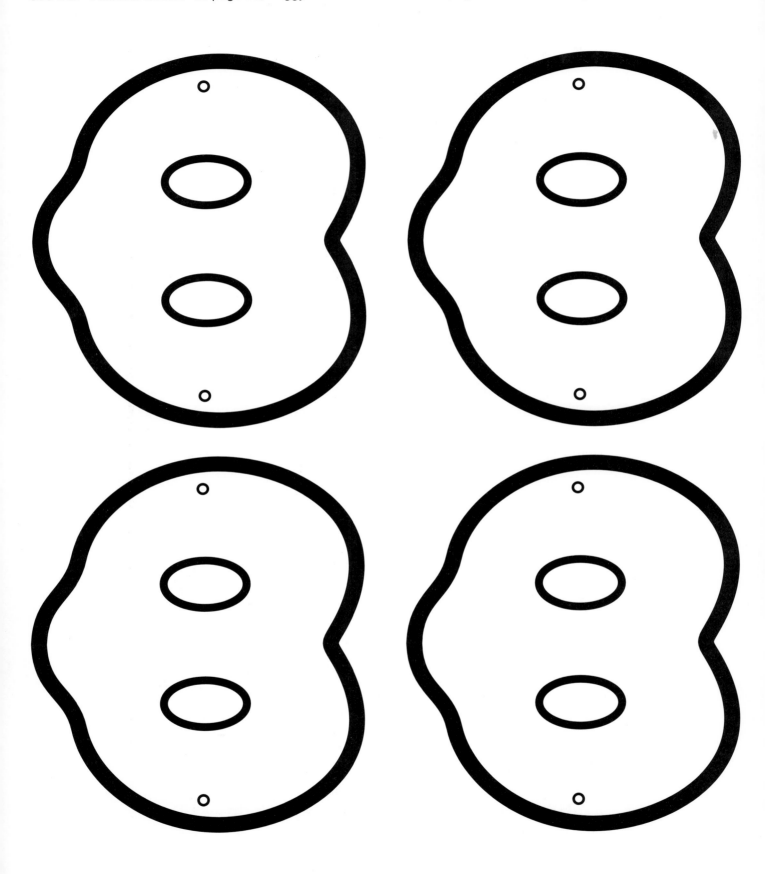

GREAT PIG PICKS AT THE LIBRARY

The Piggy in the Puddle
Written by Charlotte Pomerantz

A Treeful of Pigs
Written by Arnold Lobel

The Three Little Pigs
Retold by James Marshall

Perfect the Pig
Written by Susan Jeschke

Mrs. Potter's Pig
Written by Phyllis Root

Pigs Aplenty, Pigs Galore!
Written by David McPhail

©The Education Center, Inc.

GREAT PIG PICKS AT THE LIBRARY

The Piggy in the Puddle
Written by Charlotte Pomerantz

A Treeful of Pigs
Written by Arnold Lobel

The Three Little Pigs
Retold by James Marshall

Perfect the Pig
Written by Susan Jeschke

Mrs. Potter's Pig
Written by Phyllis Root

Pigs Aplenty, Pigs Galore!
Written by David McPhail

©The Education Center, Inc.

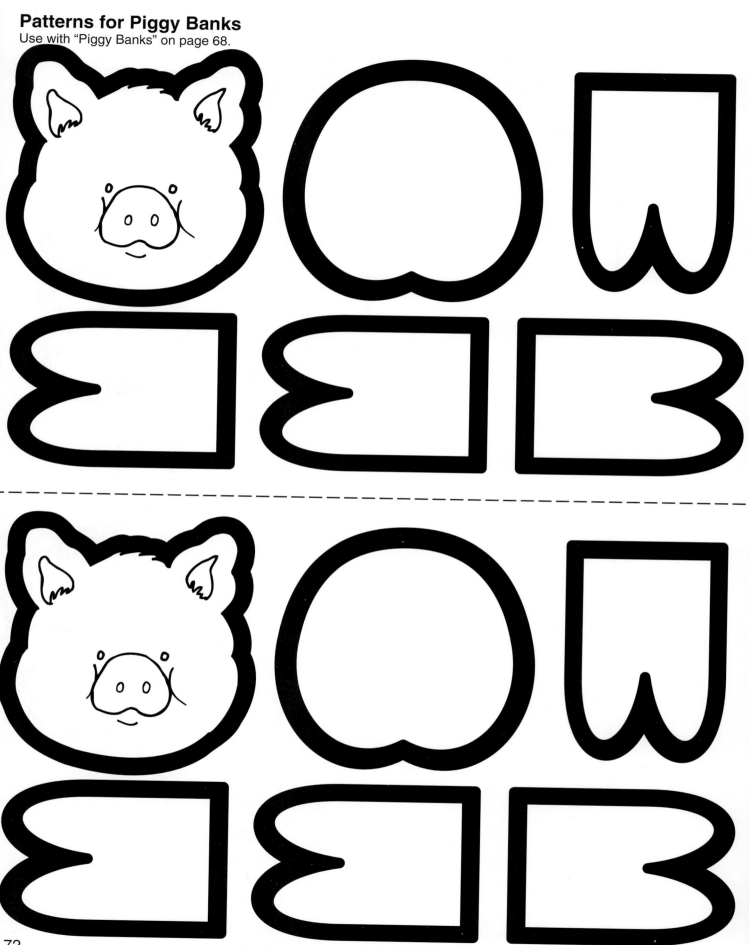

Pyramid Power

Celebrate National Nutrition Month® with a hearty helping of activities that feed the mind and promote healthful eating habits!

ideas contributed by Linda Gordetsky and Angie Kutzer

Food Riddles
Recognizing the importance of proper nutrition

Introduce your children to the topic of nutrition by using the book *What Food Is This?* by Rosmarie Hausherr. Read aloud the riddle on each page before showing children the illustration. After sharing the book, invite each child to ask her own riddle about a favorite food. Follow this activity with a discussion about the importance of food. Explain that everyone needs a certain amount of food each day in order to grow and be active. Getting this amount of food is called *nutrition*. Inform your students that all food can be sorted into six groups. Name the groups, pausing after each one to see if students can identify any food items in that group. Then let the food follies begin!

The Grub Groups
Categorizing foods by food group

Guide your students' understanding of the basic food groups with this appetizing collage display. Prepare a large outline of the Food Guide Pyramid on a bulletin board by using pushpins and colorful yarn as shown. Write each food group's title on a different colored construction paper strip and attach the strip beside its designated group's area on the display. Have each of your little ones search through magazines to find a picture of a food that he likes to eat. Instruct him to cut his choice from the magazine and return to the area in front of the display. Encourage each child to tell his classmates what he found and to name its correct group. Staple his food in its place on the display. If the display is not full of grub after everyone's turn, challenge your students to find more foods during their free time to add to the collage.

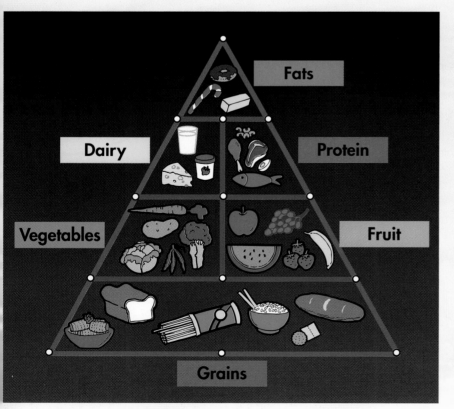

Fats

Dairy

Protein

Vegetables

Fruit

Grains

The Pyramid Poem

Identifying foods in the food pyramid

Reinforce the concept of the Food Guide Pyramid with this "munchy" masterpiece. During the first reading, point to each group on the pyramid as you spell out its specifics. Then serve more helpings of this poem and have youngsters do the pointing. (The numbers of servings noted in the poem reflect the minimum amounts needed daily.)

At the top of the pyramid
Sit lots of good treats.
But to be in good shape,
Eat just a few sweets.

The next group is dairy—
Milk, yogurt, and cheese.
For strong teeth and bones,
Eat two helpings of these.

Next to dairy are proteins—
Fish, eggs, nuts, and meat.
Two servings for energy;
These foods can't be beat.

Below is the fruit group
Full of vitamin C.
Two servings are needed
To keep you healthy.

Beside are the vegetables.
They're plants that we crunch.
To get lots of fiber,
Three servings we munch.

And, finally, the grain group—
Breads, pasta, and rice.
Eat six or more servings
Of these to feel nice!

Nutrition All Around

Increasing awareness of food, developing fine-motor skills

Provide lots of hands-on experiences for your little ones by including the following food props in your learning centers during this unit:

Building Area: Stuff empty food boxes and containers with paper, and encourage the construction of pyramid shapes!

Sand Table: Fill the table with sand, potting soil, or rice. Bury a variety of plastic veggies and invite children to dig them up with hand tools used for gardening.

Dramatic-Play Area: Create a restaurant atmosphere with chef hats, order pads, aprons, menus, and play food.

Math Area: Wash and dry empty milk cartons, and label each one with a numeral. Provide a box of straws for counting practice and matching numerals to sets.

Art Area: Encourage the making of sweet treats! Fill this center with colored play dough, cookie cutters, rolling pins, and cupcake liners.

Reading Area: Roll over a play shopping cart full of good literature on the subject of food!

The Sensational Six!

Knowing the six food groups is important for obtaining good nutrition and balancing meals. Use these activities to focus on each food group.

The Grain Train

Pam Crane

Grains Are Great! 💻
Sorting types of grain

To prepare, enlarge and duplicate the train patterns on page 82 so that each child has one engine and three cars. Mix together a box of pasta, a box of rice, and a box of cereal. Put this mixture into bowls for your children to share. Cut a construction paper strip that measures 6" x 18" for each child. Bring in a bowl of flour.

To begin this activity, have each child rub some flour between his thumb and fingers in order to feel its texture. Explain that this flour is actually a type of grass seed that has been ground into a powdery mixture. Refer back to the Food Guide Pyramid and have children name things that are made from grain. Then instruct your students to color and cut the train engine and cars from the paper. Have students assemble and glue their trains onto their construction paper strips. Then encourage your little ones to sort and glue the rice, pasta, and cereal onto the separate cars. All aboard the Grain Train!

Milk in my cheese

Dairy Delights
Developing knowledge of dairy products

Emphasize the milk content in dairy products by making these "moo-velous" milk books. To prepare, obtain a classroom supply of small milk cartons. Open their tops and wash them out. When they are dry, cut the front and back panels from the cartons. To make the booklet pages, trace around the front panel of a carton four times on a sheet of paper. Program three of the pages with "Milk in my _____." Program the fourth page with "Milk is good for you!" Duplicate this master copy for each child.

To set the "moo-ood" for milk, read *No Moon, No Milk!* by Chris Babcock. After the story, direct your youngsters' attention back to the Food Guide Pyramid collage. Explain that all dairy products contain milk and that milk helps to make teeth and bones strong. Have your little ones name some dairy products. Distribute the photocopied sheet and the panels from one carton to each of your children. Instruct her to cut the pages apart and illustrate a different dairy product on each of the first three pages. On the last page, have her draw herself drinking a big glass of milk. When each child is finished, write her dictation on each page, arrange the pages between the panels, and staple the booklet at the top. Encourage your little ones to take their booklets home to share with their families.

Please Pass the Proteins!
Understanding the benefits of protein

Have your children imagine that they are cars. Ask them what they need to make them run. Accept all reasonable answers and stop when the answer is "Gas." Then ask what happens to them when they're all out of gas. Explain that the body needs food just like a car needs gas. *Protein* is one of the substances in food that provides gas, or energy, for the body. Refer to the Food Guide Pyramid display and name some foods that are rich in protein.

Teach your little ones the following rhyme. Invite each child to say the two-line stanza alone, filling in the blank with his favorite protein. Repeat the first verse together after each child's turn.

Eggs, nuts, meat, and fish.
Eggs, nuts, meat, and fish.
Put some protein on your dish.
Pick eggs, nuts, meat, or fish!

I like [protein food]; yes I do.
I eat proteins; how 'bout you?

Palatable Plants
Comparing fruits and vegetables

The fruit and vegetable groups are similar in that they both contain foods that are plant parts. The horticultural difference is that *vegetables* may be the roots, leaves, stems, bulbs, or seeds of plants that have to be replanted annually; and *fruits* are the fleshy tissue containing the seeds of plants that live for more than two years without being replanted (perennials). Simplify this definition for children's understanding by saying that both fruits and vegetables are foods from plants; and fruits usually taste sweet.

For this fruit and veggie activity, enlarge and duplicate the mouse pattern on page 82 for each child. Discuss with your children the importance of eating fruits and vegetables because of all the vitamins and minerals that they contain. Share the book *Lunch* by Denise Fleming with your children. Stop after each item the mouse eats, and ask your little ones if the item is a fruit or vegetable. Show the picture of the messy mouse on the last page and review what it ate. Encourage your children to name other fruits and vegetables that are the same colors. Hand each child a mouse pattern, and instruct him to color the mouse according to what fruits and vegetables he wants it to eat for dinner. Label each child's picture with his own menu to resemble the picture from the book. Display these pictures on a board with a paper-plate border and add the title "Dinnertime!"

Fat in the Hat

Creating an awareness of foods high in fat, increasing visual memory

Show your little ones where the fats, oils, and sweets are located on the pyramid. Explain that they occupy the smallest part of the pyramid, to remind us to eat only a few. Bring in a hat full of items from this group—such as a candy bar, a snack-size bag of chips, an empty butter container, a soft-drink can, and a small bag of candy—and explain why each item belongs in this group. Play the following game with these items to improve problem-solving and visual-memory skills: Display the items and the hat on a tabletop. Ask a child to close his eyes while you hide one item under the hat. Invite the child to open his eyes and try to name the fat that's under the hat. Depending on the age group, you can add more items to increase the difficulty. Play until everyone has had a turn.

Not Again! 💻

Developing healthy eating habits

Use this game to help your children learn that variety is important in their diets. To prepare the game, make two identical sets of the food cards on page 81. Cut them apart and laminate them for durability. Place each set of the cards in a separate lunch bag.

To play, have two children sit across from one another, each holding a bag. To start, the children say, "Let's eat!" Each child reaches into his bag and pulls out one card. If the cards match, the children say, "Not again!", and the cards go back into the bags. If the cards do not match, the children say, "Mmmmm, something different!", and the cards stay on the table. Play continues in the same manner until all cards are on the table. Variety is the spice of life!

Skip to My Food! 💻

Identifying a food by picture and name

This circle game will burn a few calories as your children skip around to improve their matching skills. Make multiple copies of a few of the food cards on page 81 so that each child has one. Cut out and then color each card, making sure the same foods look identical. Have your little ones stand in a circle. Distribute a card to each child and ask him to hold it so that the picture faces the outside of the circle. Choose one child to skip around the circle while singing the following song, inserting her food card's name where appropriate:

(sung to the tune of "Skip to My Lou")
I eat [food name]; so do you.
I eat [food name]; so do you.
I eat [food name]; so do you.
Tasty [food name]—good for you!

As she skips and sings, instruct the child to look at the other cards and find a child holding a match to her card. Have her tap him. He joins her in skipping and singing the verse again, looking for anyone else with a matching card. When all the matches have been found, collect their cards and choose a child holding a different card to skip. Play until the students run out of cards or energy—whichever comes first!

At the Most 🖥

Sorting foods by food group, showing an understanding of maximum servings

Your little ones will practice matching, counting, and sorting in this nutrition activity. To prepare, duplicate the cards on page 81 so that there are two picture cards for fats, three cards for proteins, three cards for dairy, four cards for fruits, five cards for vegetables, and eleven cards for grains. Place these cards in a mixing bowl. On each of six index cards, write one of the following numbers: 2, 3, 3, 4, 5, and 11. Seat your children in front of a pocket chart. Put the number cards in a row at the bottom of the chart; then put one card from each food group into the chart (in its own row) to start the sorting. Invite each child to come forward, pick a card from the bowl, and place it in the correct row according to its food group. When all cards are sorted, have your children count each row and name the food group. Then direct one child to find the matching number and place it at the end of the row. Explain to your young eaters that these numbers and pictures show the *most* of a particular food group that should be eaten each day.

At the Least

Practicing healthy eating habits, recording food choices

To promote more healthful eating habits and balanced meals, make your children Keeping Track pockets. To make a pocket, cut a four-inch strip from the tab side of a letter-size file folder. Then cut the file folder in half as shown, making two folders. To make a pocket, open each folder, fold 1 1/2 inches from the bottom of the folder up, and staple the sides. Label the front of the mini folder "Keeping Track." Write "Eat It" on the left pocket and "Ate It" on the right pocket. Have children decorate the outsides of their folders by printing with vegetables, fruits, or pasta pieces dipped in paint.

Cut two-inch-square cards from colored construction paper that matches the colors of the titles on the Food Guide Pyramid display from "The Grub Groups" on page 74. Each child will need the following cards: one fat, two proteins, two dairy, two fruits, three vegetables, and six grains. These cards represent the *minimum* number of daily servings that a child needs from each of the food groups in order to maintain a balanced diet. When the paints on the folders have dried, place the servings cards in the "Eat It" pocket.

The next day, hand the folders to your children. Ask each child to tell what he ate for breakfast, and assist him in moving the corresponding cards over to the "Ate It" pocket. Do this again with your little ones after lunch and snacktime. Encourage your students to take their folders home and tell their parents about healthful eating. Challenge your little nutritionists to move the remaining servings cards to the "Ate It" pocket by eating the needed foods for dinner.

Parents and the Pyramid
Strengthening the home-school connection

For little ones, parents are the ones who are ultimately responsible for their balanced nutrition. Give parents a chance to ponder nutritional needs with this take-home activity. Fill in the blank on the parent letter from page 83 with a day that fits your schedule. Reproduce the letter on cardstock paper and send home a copy with each child. When the pyramids have been returned, review them with your group. For added impact, display the pyramids as mobiles. Cut a classroom supply of small triangles from construction paper and label each one with a child's name. Tape four of the pyramids together as shown. Thread a long string through the top and tape the end to the back of one of the pieces. Punch a hole at the bottom of each pyramid and at the top of each triangle. Tie each child's triangle onto his pyramid. Hang these mobiles in your room for a reminder to eat healthful foods.

You've Learned It; Now Eat It!
Following directions, participating in healthy eating

Wrap up your nutrition unit with this edible pyramid snack. Prepare and arrange the needed ingredients and utensils. Discuss the directions with your group; then encourage your little ones to make this food-groups treat. Dig in!

Pyramid Pie

Ingredients for One:
1 triangle of refrigerated crescent roll dough
1 tbsp. of marshmallow creme
1 tbsp. of drained fruit cocktail
1 tsp. of shredded carrots
walnut pieces
whipped topping

Directions for Each Student:
1. Place the triangle of dough on a piece of foil.
2. Spread marshmallow creme over the dough.
3. Put on the fruit cocktail, carrots, and nuts.
4. Ask your teacher to bake your snack for 11–13 minutes at 325°F.
5. Let it cool. Add a spoonful of whipped topping.
6. Eat!

Food Cards

Use with "Skip to My Food!" and "Not Again!" on page 78 and "At the Most" on page 79.

candy bar

french fries

milk

cheese

chicken

steak

egg

broccoli

carrots

corn

apple

banana

cereal

bread

rice

pear

Train Patterns
Use with "Grains Are Great!" on page 76.

The Grain Train

Mouse Pattern
Use with "Palatable Plants" on page 77.

Dear Family,

If you ask your child what a pyramid is, he or she is more likely to tell you about food groups than about an Egyptian structure. We are learning about the Food Guide Pyramid and making healthful food choices. Please cut out the pyramid from this letter, and assist your child in writing his or her name on the back. On Saturday or Sunday morning, take a moment after breakfast to help your child color in a circle for each type of food eaten during that morning's meal. Do the same for lunch, snacks, and dinner that day. The number of circles in each section represents the maximum number of servings in that food group that a child should eat each day.

Now you have a good idea of how your child's diet measures up to the national standard. Please send the completed pyramid back to us on _____. We are going to make a display of these in our classroom.

(date)

Thank you for your cooperation!

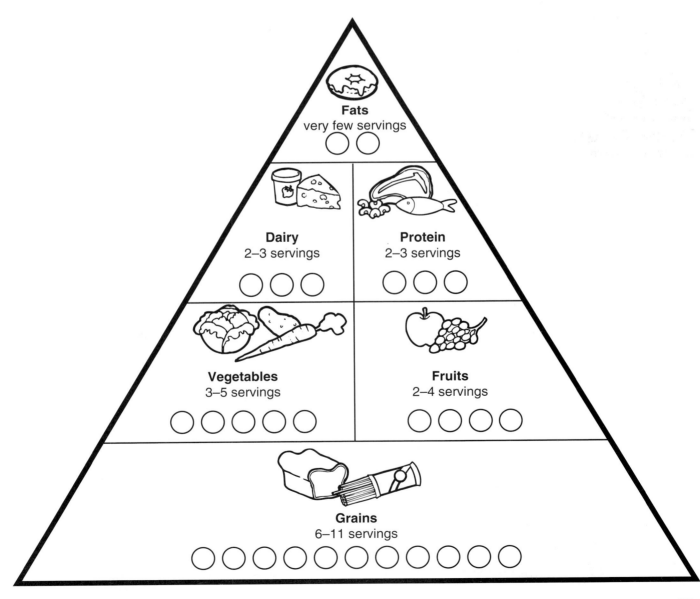

CIRCUS TIME

Step right up! The circus is in town and these fun-filled, age-appropriate activities are certain to have your youngsters flying across the curriculum with the greatest of ease.

ideas contributed by Carrie Lacher and Mackie Rhodes

The Great Announcement
Building on prior knowledge

Hear ye! Hear ye! Plan a class Circus Day, and enjoy the building anticipation and excitement as little ones help spread the news with announcements about the big event. Make one copy of the announcement on page 90; then program it with the appropriate information for your class Circus Day. Make a copy of the programmed announcement for each child. Then, for each group of three or four students, enlarge and duplicate the announcement onto a large sheet of construction paper.

Guide students to discuss what they know about a circus. Then tell youngsters that the class will be preparing to have a circus of their own. Have each child color his individual copy of the announcement as he desires. Put these aside to send home later (see "The Grand Finale" on page 88).

Then divide your class into groups of three to four students. Invite each group to embellish a copy of the enlarged announcement with brightly colored markers, glitter, and sequins to create an eye-appealing wall poster. After the posters are completed, ask students to help display them in your classroom and in the hallway.

A Day of Circus Life 🖥
Making a personal connection

Youngsters will enjoy creating a class book after being introduced to *The Circus Alphabet* by Linda Bronson. In advance, enlarge and duplicate the announcement on page 90 on a sheet of tagboard. Cut out the circus-tent shape; then trace the cutout on a large sheet of construction paper to create a book page for each child. Trace and cut out two additional circus-tent shapes to serve as book covers.

After reading the story, encourage each student to imagine herself living in a circus environment. Have her cut out her book page and then illustrate her favorite circus activity or responsibility. Write her dictated description on the page. Stack the completed pages between the covers and staple the book along the left edge. Write the title "Circus Life" on the front cover; then place the book in the reading center for youngsters to enjoy.

A Circus Day 🖥
Developing listening skills

Prepare youngsters for some of the sights of a circus with this flannelboard rhyme. Duplicate page 93 for later use. If desired, also duplicate pages 91 and 92 for use in "Circus Construction" on page 89. Then laminate and cut out the flannelboard figures on pages 91 and 92. Attach the hook side of a piece of Velcro® to the back of each flannelboard piece. In turn, invite a different student to place each corresponding figure on the flannelboard while this rhyme is recited.

Under the big top on circus day,
One little **clown** tumbles out to play.
Out trot the **horses and riders** galore.
Here come the **acrobats.** Look! There's more!
Parading **elephants.** Tame **lions,** too.
The **band** toots their horns—root-a-toot-toot!
The **ringmaster** enters—coattails, top hat.
It's a three-ring circus. Imagine that!
Lots of glitter and spangles, laughs and fun.
Candy and popcorn and hot dogs in buns.
I love the circus—excitement and noise!
The circus is here! Come on, girls and boys!

The Big Top
Using prior knowledge

Convert your classroom into a circus arena with an eye-catching big-top decoration. Die-cut a large construction paper star (or duplicate a five-inch star pattern) for each child. Then use an opaque projector to enlarge the star on a sheet of colored poster board, and cut it out. Print "Star Circus Presents..." on the poster board cutout. Ask each child to name an act, an animal, or a thing that might be seen at a circus. Write, or have the child write, his response on his construction paper star. Invite each student to decorate the edges of his star with glitter crayons, glitter, or sparkling sequins. Display the large star on an open wall in your classroom. Attach shiny, colorful streamers between the stars, draping the streamers along the wall so they resemble the form of a circus tent. Then attach the students' stars randomly along the streamers. The big top is raised! The circus will soon begin!

It's Circus Time 🖥

Reciting and dramaticizing a chant

Teach little ones this bouncy chant and its hand motions to use as a call to youngsters to come and join the circus excitement.

(sung to the tune of "Ram-Sam-Sam")

It's circus time.
(Tap imaginary watch on wrist.)

It's circus time.
(Tap imaginary watch on wrist.)

Come to the big top.
(Bring hands together over head to form tent.)

It's circus time.
(Tap imaginary watch on wrist.)

(Repeat the first verse.)

The show is beginning.
See the tumblers and silly clowns,
The jugglers and trainers,
Horses and riders bumping up and down.

(Repeat the first verse twice.)

Watch seals, birds, and monkeys.
Hoop-jumping dogs and dancing bears,
Big elephants marching,
Lions and tigers leaping over chairs.

(Repeat the first verse twice.)

Send in the Clowns

Identifying feelings that result from given situations

No circus would be complete without the silly, sad, and slaphappy clowns. Invite your students to create a convertible clown mask that will allow them ample opportunity to explore and express some different emotions as they role-play circus clowns. To make a mask, duplicate the clown mask and mouth patterns on page 93 on a sheet of tagboard for each child. Help the child cut out the mouth, the mask, and the eyeholes; then have him decorate the cutouts as desired. Have the child position the mouth cutout on the front of the mask. Then help him secure the mouth to the mask with a brad. Attach a piece of tape over the extended brad tabs to prevent the child from getting scratched. Then have the child attach the end of a wide craft stick to the bottom of the mask. To use the mask, describe to students a situation that might elicit a happy or sad response, such as receiving a bag of cotton candy or missing the circus due to illness. Ask each child to turn the mouth on his mask to indicate his response to that situation—a smile or a frown. Then have him hold the mask up to his face.

After exploring happy and sad emotions, invite youngsters to take turns selecting dress-up items from a clown prop box. Encourage them to role-play clown acts to represent the two different emotions depicted on their masks.

We're Having a Ball!
Increasing visual discrimination, developing eye-hand coordination

Jugglers combine skill and a quick eye as they toss and catch their juggling props. Invite youngsters to do the same in a modified juggling act. To prepare, collect a supply of soft foam balls to use as juggling balls. Use a permanent marker to program pairs of balls with identical numerals, shapes, or figures. Or program each pair with corresponding uppercase and lowercase letters. Place an empty basket at one end of the classroom and a basket containing one ball from each pair at the opposite end of the room. Put the remaining balls in a box near the empty basket.

Divide your class into two-person juggling teams. Invite each child from one team to stand near one of the baskets. Have the child standing by the empty basket close his eyes and pick a ball from the box. Instruct him to toss the ball to his juggling partner. When the partner receives the ball, have him find the corresponding ball in his basket and then toss each of the balls, one at a time, back to his partner. Encourage that child to check the balls for a correct match and then place them in his basket. Continue play, having the partners switch positions periodically until all the matches are found. Then reset the game and invite another juggling team to play.

At the Tip of the Nose
Increasing visual discrimination

Jugglers aren't the only circus performers who use balls—seals are also quite amazing to watch as they balance balls on the tips of their noses. Give youngsters the opportunity to seal their matching skills while imitating a ball-balancing skill in this learning center. In advance, cut a short slit under the programmed skill on each ball prepared in "We're Having a Ball!" Put all the balls in a box in a center. Place a basket in front of a mirror in the center. When a child visits the center, encourage him to sort through the box to find a set of matching balls. For fun, have him balance each ball on his nose—in circus seal fashion—by slipping the slit of the ball over the tip of his nose. Invite the child to watch his own balancing act in the mirror. Then have him drop the ball off his nose and into the basket.

Up on the High Wire
Developing balance, following directions

When students engage in this balancing act, they will experience a sampling of the skill needed by performers who walk the tightrope. Place a long, thin tape line on the floor to represent the tightrope. If desired, have available a child's umbrella with safety tips or a fat dowel as a balance prop. Invite each child in turn to walk the tightrope according to your directions, such as on tiptoe, with a heel-to-toe step pattern, or backward. If he chooses, a child may use the umbrella or dowel for balance. After taking a turn, invite each child to walk the line again—this time to the words of "High Wire Artist" by Hap Palmer on the album *Easy Does It.* Youngsters will find it's not as easy as it looks!

Big-Top Treats
Following directions

Top off your circus show with a tasty treat that will enhance any circus experience. But first invite youngsters to prepare a decorative bag in which to hold their treats. To make a treat bag, have each child use a pair of child-safe edging scissors to cut a decorative edge along the top of a paper lunch bag. Then have him embellish the outside of his bag with shiny star stickers and write his name on it.

To prepare for making the treats, place buttered popcorn, small pretzels, honey-roasted peanuts, and M&M's® into separate dishes, and add a scoop to each dish. Invite each child to pour a scoopful of each desired ingredient into his bag. Instruct him to tie the bag with a length of ribbon, then shake the bag to mix the ingredients. Set the treat bags aside for later use in "The Grand Finale."

Elephants on Parade
Identifying numerals

When youngsters participate in a parade wearing their own customized elephant headbands, you can count on lots of number fun taking place. To prepare, write a different numeral from 1 to 20 on separate sheets of construction paper. Laminate the labeled sheets for durability. Randomly arrange the sheets of paper in a circle on the floor; then tape the sheets in place.

To make a headband, give each child a sentence strip, a paper plate, and an arm-length strip of gray crepe paper streamer. Have each child paint his sentence strip and paper plate with a gray paint made from a mixture of white glue and a small amount of black liquid tempera paint. Then invite him to sprinkle silver glitter onto the wet paint. After the glue dries, ask each child to cut his plate in half to create two elephant ears. Fit the sentence strip around the child's head to make a headband; then staple the ends together. Staple the paper-plate ears to opposite sides of the band and the streamer—or elephant's trunk—to the middle of the band. Fold the ears forward so that they stand out at the sides. With youngsters wearing their headbands, play a version of "Baby Elephant Walk" or other circus music. Have the elephants march around the number circle until you stop the music. Ask each child to identify the number he is standing on. Then start the music again, inviting your marching elephants to proceed with their parade.

The Grand Finale
Strengthening the home-school connection

The big top is raised, the acts have been rehearsed, and the treats are ready to be eaten. It's time for your youngsters to put on their own circus show to wrap up their circus study! A few days prior to the big event, have each child take home his announcement made in "The Great Announcement" on page 84 to share with his family. Have your class divide themselves into groups of two or three children. Encourage each group to select and practice a circus act to perform for an audience.

On Circus Day, in ringmaster fashion, invite each group to perform its act. After the last delightful performance, serve each student and visitor the circus treats from "Big-Top Treats" with a cup of punch. Serve additional light refreshments to your circus audience. Frolicking feats, fanciful fun, and finger foods—what a fantastic finale!

TIME FOR INTERMISSION

While youngsters are biding their time between circus acts, engage them in some of these intermission activities to promote cross-curricular skill development.

Geometric Circus
Using a variety of art media

Engage youngsters in some clowning around with shapes. To begin, read aloud *Circus* by Lois Ehlert. Then provide an assortment of construction paper cutouts in various sizes and shapes—circles, squares, triangles, rectangles, ovals, and stars. Invite each child to assemble a clown, or another circus character, on a sheet of construction paper using the shape cutouts. For added interest, have hole punchers available for student use. Label each child's creation with his dictated name for it; then display these pictures on a bulletin board titled "Geometric Circus."

Carrie

Silly the Clown

Circus Construction 💻
Working cooperatively, role-playing

Youngsters will build their spatial relations and problem-solving abilities as they build structures for a model circus grounds. To make blocks for this activity, gather an assortment of boxes in different sizes and shapes. Cover each box with construction paper or decorative Con-Tact® covering. Attach each of the flannelboard figures made in "A Circus Day" on page 85 to a separate block. Or duplicate the copies of pages 91 and 92 as many times as necessary to provide a picture for each block; then color and cut out the pictures. Attach a different picture to each block. Then invite youngsters to use items in your block center to set up a circus grounds and use the circus blocks to role-play circus activities.

Three-Ring Reading

Circus
Written by Lois Ehlert

Emeline at the Circus
Written by Marjorie Priceman

Harold's Circus
Written by Crockett Johnson

Olivia Saves the Circus
Written by Ian Falconer

Peter Spier's Circus!
Written by Peter Spier

Use with "The Great Announcement" and "A Day of Circus Life" on page 84 and "The Grand Finale" on page 88.

IT'S CIRCUS TIME!

Food, Frolic, Fancy Feats, and Fun.
A Little Something for Everyone!

Please join us for the big event:

Date: _____

Time: _____

Place: _____

Flannelboard Figures

Use with "A Circus Day" on page 85 and "Circus Construction" on page 89.

Flannelboard Figures

Use with "A Circus Day" on page 85 and "Circus Construction" on page 89.

Clown Mask and Mouth Patterns
Use with "Send in the Clowns" on page 86.

Cut out.

Cut out.

Index